# BALTIMORE CATECHISM: CLEAN SLATE

*(THE FALL AND RISE OF A CATHOLIC BOY)*

By John T. Hourihan Jr.

*Aster Press*
*An imprint of Blue Fortune Enterprises*

BALTIMORE CATECHISM: CLEAN SLATE
The Fall and Rise of a Catholic Boy

Copyright © 2020 by John Hourihan

All rights reserved. Printed in the United States of America. No part of this book may be used or reproduced in any manner whatsoever without written permission except in the case of brief quotations embodied in critical articles or reviews.

For information contact :
Blue Fortune Enterprises, LLC
Aster Press
P.O. Box 554
Yorktown, VA 23690
http://blue-fortune.com


Book and Cover design by Wesley Miller, WAMCreate, wamcreate.co
Cover Photo by John T. Hourihan, Jr.

ISBN: 978-1-948979-52-8

First Edition: December 2020

## Other Titles by John Hourihan

The Mustard Seed: 2130

The Mustard Seed: 2110

The Mustard Seed: 2095

Beyond the Fence: Converging Memoirs (with author Amanda Eppley)

Baseball: Play Fair and Win

Parables for a New Age

*Praise for Baltimore Catechism:*

The narrator meets life's difficulties with an equanimity unusual in a six-year-old, and that is the book's charm. No wounded soul here; though he lives with poverty and occasional violence, such elements are but threads in the larger tapestry of his life. That life is nurtured and sustained by his rowdy extended family, especially his mother, and, eventually, the gift of religion.

Karen Cavalli, author of *Bad Mind*, *Undercover Goddess* and *Down*.

John Hourihan's *Baltimore Catechism: Clean Slate* is a charming account of a precocious child's struggle with his Catholic school first grade year. This fictionalized memoir tells how the boy John struggles with the contradictions in Catholic teachings and the difficulties his family faces. The writing is lively and insightful.

Robert Archibald, author of *Roundabout Revenge*, *Guilty Until Proven Innocent* and *Who Dung It*.

This book is a gem. This story of a young Irish boy trying to understand the seeming difference between religion and reality is laugh out loud funny. But you don't have to be Irish or Catholic to enjoy this nostalgic journey into the past as he struggles to do the right thing.

Patti Gaustad Procopi, author of *Please… Tell Me More*

As a fellow writer of semi-autobiographic fiction, I applaud John Hourihan's new book, *Baltimore Catechism*. Told with the innocence of childhood and the tongue-in cheek irony of adulthood, the book brings out the conflict between religion and reality. Through the eyes of a young Irish-American boy, the book explores what it means to be religious. The author's sardonic whit, coupled with his poignant visual, auditory and olfactory images of people, places and events, makes the book an enticing read. This book is a paean to our common humanity and to what is good in all of us.

Christian Pascale, author of *Memories Are The Stories We Tell Ourselves* and *Windows of Heaven*.

*This book is fiction but based on a true story.*

*Many of the names and identifying factors have been changed to ensure the privacy of individuals. Some of the characters are composites of several different people, and any similarities to actual people are coincidental.*

## Dedication

This book is dedicated to my wife Linda, whose faith and love for everyone has always astounded me; to my mother Genevieve, who taught us the truth about right and wrong; and to my sister Nancy, who always had my back.

# PART I
# The Creed

# CHAPTER 1
Innocence in Eden

**IT WAS A TIME OF** enlightenment into what had never in my life been dark.

The comfort of the perfect green and lazy summer was over, and the moment had come for the long-feared first-grade bus ride. My mother and I were both more than a little nervous because of what had happened when I last attempted this.

I stood straight, shoulders back, as she knelt and preened over me in the living room while my four older sisters fought for space in front of the bathroom mirror like hummingbirds on a pansy. My brother Dennis, too young for school, was still asleep. I was to wear my tan corduroys, red and blue striped jersey, and socks that matched each other. She spit on her hand and tried to make the cowlick in the back of my mouse brown hair stay down. Giving up in vain, she looked into my right eye, squinting a bit with worry.

She looked nervous.

Last year, at four and a half years old, I had gone through this ritual to prepare for kindergarten. She had packed me onto the bus and waved goodbye from the top of the dirt driveway that snaked from our home, through the woods, and to the road that led to town. I dutifully waved back to her even though it had been a beautiful September day in New England, and she was forcing me to leave my idyllic life of wildflowers, black raspberries, stone walls, crow calls, chiding squirrels, and the endless natural beauty of the fields, woods, and the lake behind my home. Feeling betrayed, I let my head bounce gently against the window with the bumps from the road.

Love was not a choice. It was a given. Parents loved their children, and children loved their parents, no holds barred, no matter what, so I still felt the love I had at being by her side mixed with the anxiety that I would be away from her protection all day inside a building downtown miles from the beautiful creation that surrounded my cedar-shingled hovel in the forest.

At this time, a year ago, I had had other ideas. Kindergarten began at eight a.m. At ten minutes after eight, Miss Lawler threw away my apple because I was "eating at an inappropriate time." I wasn't ready for there to be an appropriate time to eat an apple in autumn, so by nine a.m., Jimmy's shiny green taxi crunched down the gravel and dirt drive and stopped in the hard dirt of the front yard where cars turned around. My mother, in a tan skirt and white blouse, appeared at the door. With her brunette hair wrapped in her pale blue work kerchief, she wiped her hands on the flowered apron one of my sisters had made her for last Christmas and gazed perplexed at the taxi until I pushed open the back door of the cab and stepped out onto the driveway. I smiled, having been returned to my paradise, as Butch the cat peered at me from under the makeshift plank bench beside the front door.

"I'm sorry, Gen," Jimmy said, "but he said you would pay me when we got here?"

He posed it as a question since he was a friend and knew with the food bill for six kids at the advent of the 1950s my family had little money to spare. The adults had looked at each other in dumbfounded silence for a few seconds.

"How old is he?" Jimmy asked as he leaned out of the driver side window.

"Four," my mother laughed.

"Amazing," Jimmy replied. "I guess he just walked out of school, down to the stand, had to cross Main Street and stepped in the door and announced, '197 Purchase Street. My mother will pay you when we get there.' Then he went outside and got into the cab."

"How much?"

"Thirty-five cents?"

She went back into the kitchen and returned with the money. In this way, kindergarten at the public school had ended. I would be trusted to go to the first grade at St Mary's Central Catholic Grammar School the next year. My entry into concentrated Catholicism, a forced alteration in my DNA, was to take place today.

She held my shoulders and looked into my eyes. Her perpetual smile faltered for an instant, and she said, "Now, you stay at school until they let you out, you hear? Learn what they have to teach you. It's the way it has to be. It's the law. You don't want to get arrested yet, do you?"

I promised to be good, but I wasn't happy that my beloved mother would willingly send me away against my will to learn from people who didn't understand that I already had a perfect world, and a pet squirrel who ate from my hand. And what was it I was supposed to learn at this building with the flesh of cold granite and the Murphy-oil-soaped wooden skeleton?

As all those of us who had been picked up by the bus on Purchase Street trudged toward the school, I saw one for the first time—a nun, a Sister of Saint Joseph. Everyone in my family, from my sisters to my grandmother, had told me how wonderful these women of God were. I, therefore, revered them even before I knew what one looked like. Life was like that in the time of Pope Pius XII, Eisenhower, and Howdy Doody.

She stood tall on the top granite step of the entrance. She

was dressed from head to toe in black. "Like the witch in my Little Lulu funny book," I thought. She even wore a black veil that covered the back of her head and draped down the sides. Her forehead was wrapped with a starched white cardboardey thing. There was an equally starched white bib covering her chest, and a six-inch silver cross, large enough to have been a weapon, hung around her neck from a thick gold chain. Another cross of the same imposing size hung from a lariat-like rosary, double-looped from her belt to her knee. A little man was nailed to each cross, and I thought, "I hope these people like me." Her black gown trailed almost to the ground of the step, leaving only enough room for me to see her club-like black shoes. I thought that someone might have warned me what my warders were going to look like. My first religious experience, it turned out, was to be sheer fright.

I'm sure the nuns felt the same way.

I was a sight rarely seen.

More than a year before my entry into the first grade, I had fallen down the stairs from the attic to the first floor of our house, cracking all my teeth. The dentist had told my parents how much it would cost for him to take care of them, and when they winced at the amount as if someone had just pulled one of their teeth, he offered a new idea. He said, "They are baby teeth. You could give him all the candy he wants and let them fall out." I thought it was a great idea. What he didn't explain was that first, the teeth would rot.

My smile had become a maw of pain and black fangs.

In addition, in showing my brother Dennis how to take pain, I had pulled out a clump of hair which left me looking like a child experiencing pattern baldness on the left side of my head. About the same time, I had also happened on a pair of tweezers in the bathroom. My older sister Nancy said they were to "pull out your eyebrows." I tried it. I pulled out my eyebrows, both of them, forcing my mother to draw in my missing brows with a Maybelline make-up pencil. When I inspected them in the bathroom mirror, I noticed she had put them a little high on my forehead, and I looked as if I was in a perpetual state of surprise.

I wore a pair of glasses to my first day of school because of my lazy eye. One side had a lens as thick as a Coke-bottle bottom that made my right eye seem extraordinarily large, and the other side was covered with a black patch. I looked for all the world like the spawn of a Cyclops.

It wasn't uncommon that when I met people for the first time, they stepped back a step to reassess, as if they had just been punched. And because of my closeness with my father, my vocabulary was that of an Irish pieceworker at a shoe shop.

I clutched my lunch bag and walked toward the door. The nun looked down at me silently for a second or two. I thought I saw her wince a bit, and then she said, "Get in line." I hadn't noticed that all the other kids formed a two-by-two line, and I thought, "How the hell did they know to do that?"

"Now!" she said, so I did.

Catholic school and I were not a match made in heaven, but I wasn't aware of that as I arrived confidently for first grade.

# CHAPTER 2
## The Purpose of Man's Existence

*THE BALTIMORE CATECHISM* **WAS LAID** on each lift-top desk in front of each of the thirty-two children in Sister Thomas Joseph's classroom one morning in about the third week of school. I could read, thanks to my older sister Patricia, but many of the trapped children looked at each other or at the nun in horror.

Their frightened faces said, "Was I supposed to know how to read?"

Little did they know that the next book we would get would be named *Streets and Roads,* and this new book would teach us the mundane talent of reading about Dick and Jane and Sally and Spot the dog. It was with this book we learned to "Sound it out," and soon a few of us would be laughing in the back of the room while sounding out the words "fought" and "sought" as "fogit" and "sogit."

While we were contemplating what the purpose was of these dark blue covered books from Baltimore, where the Orioles played, Sister cleared her throat and spoke, just one syllable.

"One!"

We stood as a unit from our bolted down wooden seats, much like the conditioned response of Pavlov's dogs. I was wondering if the Baltimore team was named after the bird or the bird after the team.

"Two," she continued. I settled on the bird being named after the team, since the team was much more important.

We turned together to face the back of the room.

"Three."

We all scurried up onto our chairs. Kneeling on the seat, we used the chair back for support until we were stable. I had figured out on the second day that it was a good idea to spread my knees a few extra inches wider than normal for balance. When we reached stability, we released our death grip on the chair back, placed our hands palm-to-palm, fingers pointed to heaven, in front of our angelic faces, or in my case I looked more demonic than angelic. Then we closed our eyes, in my case, my eye, and made ready to recite our lessons.

With the wisdom of the Holy Ghost invisible at her back, Sister jumped off the precipice and fully into teaching first-graders what they would have to know about being a

Catholic in 1951.

"Who made us, children?"

"God made us, Sister," we answered in unison. And so it began.

Studying these early pages of the book was a communal effort. I incorporated help from my whole family. At home, I read the book line by line, and they quizzed me on it. I'm sure many of my classmates had someone read it to them; therefore, not what they read but what they heard was what they learned, rendering the God of all things a "supreme bean" as opposed to our own "human beanness." Sort of like pole beans and string beans in our garden, only human and supreme.

Later in that school day, flipping pages of the new book past where we had so far read, we would find from the pictures that God was apparently a giant head with a white beard who hovered in the clouds and who looked down on us from above.

"Who is God?"

"God is the Supreme Bean, infinitely perfect, who made all things and keeps them in existence, Sister."

"Why did God make us?"

"God made us to show forth His goodness and to share with us His everlasting happiness in heaven, Sister."

"What must we do to gain the happiness of heaven?"

"To gain the happiness of heaven, we must know, love, and serve God in this world, Sister."

"From whom do we learn to know, love, and serve God?"

"We learn to know, love, and serve God from Jesus Christ, the Son of God, who teaches us through the Catholic Church, Sister."

Wearing underwear wasn't something I did all the time, and this new stuff was bothering me, being bunched unnaturally into places it shouldn't have been. First, I tried to wiggle it free. It didn't work, so I was forced to reach back and… without warning, she rustled up the aisle and whacked my hand with a black, rubber-tipped wooden pointer. Then she returned to her place in front of the exit door. This was going to be even less fun than I had expected. I looked for a way out, but there was none.

"Where do we find the chief truths taught by Jesus Christ through the Catholic Church?"

"We find the chief truths taught by Jesus Christ through the Catholic Church in the Apostles' greed, Sister."

"Say the Apostles' Creed, children."

I took this time to look back over my shoulder at Sister. I knew that look. She was glaring at me as if she were someone else's mother, and I was a wicked influence on her son. I closed my eyes against her stare and chimed in with the rest of my class.

"I believe in God, the Father Almighty, Creator of heaven and earth; and in Jesus Christ, His only Son, Our Lord; who was conceived by the Holy Ghost, born of the Virgin Mary, suffered under Pontius Pilate, was crucified, died and was buried. He descended into hell; the third day He arose again from the dead; He ascended into heaven, sitteth at the right hand of God, the Father Almighty; (whose name it turned out later was Howard) from thence He shall come to judge the living and the dead. I believe in the Holy Ghost, the Holy Catholic Church, the communion of Saints, the forgiveness of sins, the resurrection of the body, and life everlasting. Amen."

"One, two, three," and we were all dutifully sitting back into our chairs. I looked at my reddened knuckles. I didn't know what I had done wrong, but I didn't see how my knuckles were going to survive this ordeal.

## CHAPTER 3
One Foot in Paradise

**THAT WEEKEND, I SAT ON** my refrigerator-sized rock behind the house, several yards to the right of the barn, enjoying the sun and staring off at the hay fields encircled by the soon to be multi-colored oaks, maples, elms, and green pines. I closed my eyes and took in the warmth of the September sun. My mother had told me to learn what I was being taught, so I wondered about what I had learned in my first weeks of school.

I watched a frightened garter snake slither from under the rock. He stopped for an instant and looked at me as if to say, "I'll be back," and then disappeared into the grass; my first thought was that if God in fact made everyone, I supposed He was responsible for my mother being "on the nest" again.

Our family currently consisted of, in order of age, Patricia, then came Diane, then the twins Nancy and Sheila, myself, Dennis, and of course my mother and father. It was obvious to me that if this supreme bean, who was all good, all knowing, and all powerful, and created everyone, was paying attention, He would know the Hourihan family already had too many kids to feed on a shoe-shop bedlaster's salary, especially when half the paycheck usually went to Tibby's Bar, the Brass Rail, or the bookies, or all three.

I spent the rest of my morning wondering what a holy ghost was, and if I was supposed to be afraid of it, and trying to figure out why the Apostle's Greed said Jesus had to go to hell, since he was God and all good and all powerful. I mean, if God had to go to hell, what chance did the rest of us have?

It seemed that every time I learned some of what they wanted to teach me, I came away saying, "Huh?"

I left the comfort of my rock and went back inside the house. The electricity was off again, so I climbed onto my bed, made a mountain of the bed sheet, dug out my army men, and had a nice plastic war.

In our four-room home in the woods, the living room was the central room. With a queen-size bed in the middle, it doubled as the girls' bedroom. It had six doors; Moving clockwise, one door went directly into the side yard, another to the sun porch, one to the Little Room where the boys slept, one to the bathroom, one to my parents' bedroom, and the last one to the pantry which connected to the kitchen.

There were times when some of the girls and some boys had to sleep in the same room, but those sleeping arrangements were all designed around who was growing breasts and who wasn't.

I found that if I turned up the volume knob on the stand-up Philco in the girls' room and then snuck down the length of the pantry, my parents in the kitchen would speak freely, expecting that we were all listening to *Front Page Farrell, My Son Jeep* or *Stella Dallas*. This way I could hear what was being said in the kitchen. I guess this was just part of my double-barrel learning experience: reality vs. religion.

From my vantage point a few days later, sitting on the pantry counter, I leaned snugly against the wall next to the opening to the kitchen. I listened to my parents talking about the things I wasn't supposed to know for a while. I guess until I "grew up."

On this particular day, they were discussing the miraculous gift from God that would turn out to be my brother Cornelius Joseph, the seventh child in the family.

"Jack, how the devil are we going to be able to pay for this?" My mother never actually swore. She left taking the Lord's name in vain to my father, who did an excellent job of it.

If this perfect God was going to show forth his goodness, I was sure we would find the money to feed everyone. As the nuns said, "The Lord will provide." Of course, that would be as long as everyone kept healthy. I wished sincerely that my parents had just a tad more faith in Howard. I guess it had been a long time since they had heard the Baltimore Orioles Catechism.

My mother sat at her seat at one end of the drop-leaf wooden kitchen table. My father, at the other end, looked out the window into the darkening dusk of the back yard. Scrapper Jack Hourihan always seemed larger than he was, and not just to his children. He was 6'1" and was only 165 pounds but most of that was heart, according to my Uncle Jim. He had hair as black as night, blue eyes, and he was exceptionally strong from sports as a boy and work as a man. In his unnaturally long list of accomplishments as an Irishman was his four-hour donnybrook with William McReedy who would eventually become the Chief of Police in town. My cousin Sean told me, "Chief Mac had fifty pounds on Uncle Jack, but they kept on fighting for four solid hours up and down the railroad tracks down by Toody's Diner up to Central Street. My father says nearly the whole town came to watch, and when the battle was over, and it was a declared a draw, no one ever messed with Scrapper Jack Hourihan again."

Tonight at the table, he turned from the darkness outside and smiled at his wife. "Well, I've been holding back a little. I can work faster. If I can do a few more cases a day, I think we can handle another kid. No sense in griping like a gurrier."

She poked her spoon into her cup of Lipton tea in silence. I could tell it was Lipton tea because, as I peeked around the corner into the kitchen, I saw the box. It had a picture on it of the bus driver guy with the handlebar mustache and the little bus-driver hat. I don't know what a bus driver had to do with tea, but there he was. I heard the plop of the Carnation canned milk into the tea, and then the spoon clinked against the sides of the cup while she stirred. I smelled the warm tea. Her silence usually meant she was going through several thoughts unspoken. "Won't that ruin the rate?" she asked.

Ruining the rate was something us piece workers knew about. If you worked too fast, the pre-union company would just lower the amount of money it would give you for each piece of work. In my father's instance that would be a case of shoes, and if he ruined the rate by speeding up, and some others couldn't keep up, everyone would lose money, and Scrapper Jack Hourihan was "the fastest bedlaster this side of the Atlantic."

"I guess they'll just have to keep up," he said.

"They're your friends, Jack. Don't do that." She sipped again at her tea, and then she said what they both must have been thinking. "Maybe stay away from the Brass Rail for a while? What do you think?"

There was no answer. My father had the Irishman's curse. He kept chugging along faster and faster, trying to catch up with the past, and when he couldn't catch up, he lubricated the rails.

I had been on my way to the kitchen to ask for an oleo and cinnamon toast, but now I decided maybe it was a bad time, so I went back hungry to listen to Gunsmoke.

As the lawman fought to rid the old West of bad guys, I remembered that as most radio listeners could not know, rather than a big tough marshal with a gun, Matt Dillon was really, as my cousin Sean had told me, a short fat guy with a microphone. For some reason that made me think that Jesus couldn't have known he was God when he was a little kid like me. He probably walked around the world with no one knowing He was the Almighty, not even Himself. I mean, I could be God and I wouldn't know it, or this baby my mother was carrying might be God, and an angel was going to tell her later. He could be Cornelius Joseph God. The two sides of my Roman Catholic childhood were so often at odds with each other. It was all very confusing, but I was determined to do it right.

The good nuns and priests became my holy conduit to God, and my family was my lifeline to reality.

# CHAPTER 4
God and His Perfections

**BY ALMOST SIX YEARS OLD,** I had already noticed that girls differed from boys in ways that were a mystery to me, and it was heartening that Elaine, Laurie, and Pansy were in the same school. The girls were children of my mother's friends, but I was especially happy that the beautiful, red-haired Linda Chandler was in the next classroom from mine. Linda's home was only a few minutes' walk through the woods, and we had spent the summer on her swings eating her grandfather's cultivated raspberries and talking incessantly about everything from religion to Crusader Rabbit. I don't know about her, but I was falling in love. I guess her mother saw this, and by the end of the summer she had told us Linda was no longer allowed to play in the woods with the rest of us. The way her mother looked at me that day, I felt I had done something wrong, but I had no idea what it was or who I did it to.

In first grade at St. Mary's I had been put in the back row of chairs, and if I craned my body just a little backward in my chair, I could see through the window in our classroom door then through the window in the door of the classroom across the hall. Sometimes I would catch a glimpse of my favorite neighbor walking to her seat. I was doing just that when Sister did her one, two, three routine, and I found myself kneeling backwards on my chair facing the back of the room but still searching through the windows that were now to my left.

As Linda walked slowly past the window of her classroom door, she smiled. I smiled back, and she was gone, so I tuned back into what the good nun had been saying. It was to be a pleasant day.

"What are some of the perfections of God, children?"

I chimed in loudly because I knew this one, but before the answer ended, I had drifted to a different thought. During these answers, sometimes a few kids said the words and the rest of us just mumbled along, like everyone did at Mass. Each Sunday we stood when others stood, knelt when others knelt, sat when other sat, and mumbled piously when we didn't know the words. As long as you genuflected all the way to the floor when you came in and left, and bowed your head when you said Jesus, everything was alright with the nuns, and therefore with God. I was impressed one Sunday when my father forgot what was going on, and the priest stopped for a second, saw my father standing while everyone else was sitting and just bellowed out, "Sit down, Jack." Then they smiled like they knew each other.

But at once I was back in class and reciting. "Some of the perfections of God are: God is internal, all-good, all-knowing, all-present, and almighty, Sister."

"Is God all-wise, all-holy, all-merciful, and all-just?"

"Yes, Sister, God is all-wise, all-holy, all-merciful, and all-just." I often thought, all just what? But I never asked.

At this point we did the one, two, three, and sat back down to learn our new lessons. Religion was the first class of every day and went as long as it took to force a thought into our collective heads. Then came math, which was ultimately less important, and then science, which was totally unimportant in the scheme of Catholic things.

Today we were learning about the Bible.

It seems this holy book was the written word of God; the instruction manual for all of us. The only problem with it was that it was not easily understood. Even according to the Baltimore Catechism book, which was the explanation of the instructions, not all of the passages were to be understood because the words had changed their meaning over time, so the only way to clarify it was through the "authority of the Catholic Church" or by decree of my grandmother.

Nonetheless, *The Baltimore Catechism* said we should read

the Bible if we wanted to understand the rules of the game. So that night I opened up the good book. My mother had bought this particular one in a box of books at an auction for a dime. There had been three Bibles in the box and a handful of what my mother called her "mystery books." Mum explained that some books were in the box because people were done reading them and some because no one wanted to read them. I assumed the Bibles had been the ones that people had finished.

In that book I found that Howard, the giant head in the clouds, hadn't just created me and all the other people. He had also created everything else; the planet, the animals, the birds. It was a bit confusing, but I liked the idea. It was nice not to be confused about the day and night, the animals and fish, and the land and sea. It was simple: God made it all for us, end of story. It was comforting to have the world stop spinning long enough to understand that this all-powerful Supreme Being built all this for humans, so we were probably pretty safe living here. Oh, right, my mother had told me God wasn't a bean, and that Howard wasn't God's name. It was confusing because our favorite prayer said, "Our Father who art in heaven, Howard be thy name," but I always believed my mother who never lied.

# CHAPTER 5
## Stepping onto the Merry-Go-Round

**THE MOST ORNATE AND DREAMED** about carousel ever built for mankind had been there at Lakeview Park for generations. It included the organ music, the carnival smell, and its actual brass ring hanging on a white and shining gilded pole off the side just out of reach, like heaven. But it was as new to me as was *The Baltimore Catechism*.

Sadly however, due to the apathy of the buying public, the day that I was introduced to it was also the first day of its dismantling. That confused me, but I trusted my father.

He woke me up early on a Saturday morning, so early that he still smelled like Pabst Blue Ribbon and cigarette smoke, the smell of the barroom where he had spent most of last night playing poker. By six I could tell the difference between the sweet and comforting smell of Pabst at Tibby's and the acrid skunk-like aroma of Rupert Knickerbocker at the Jolly Roger, so I could always tell what my old man had been drinking when I got close enough.

"Get up Jocko, you are going to love this."

After wolfing down a bowl of Cream of Wheat, I was hustled outside where Jimmy's Taxi was waiting for us. I sheepishly glanced at Jimmy in the mirror as I climbed onto the plush smoke-filled cloth back seat, and my father slid in beside me, lighting an Old Gold with a wooden match that he struck on his pant leg.

"Where we going, Jack?" Jimmy slid his glance in the mirror so he could see my old man.

"Lakeview Park."

"You sure? Isn't it closed this early?"

"Not today. Not for Jocko here."

I watched as the cab driver shuffled the cards in his head, and the one that had said, "This place is not open for hours yet," ended up on the bottom of the deck, and it was replaced with the one that said, "This is a double fare since it's in the next town," and the car lurched up the driveway to the road.

Lakeview Park had a swimming lake, dodge 'ems, paddle boats, a frighteningly high Ferris wheel, some game booths, and the carousel.

At the entrance we stepped from the taxi, Scrapper Jack asked Jimmy to wait, and we began our walk along the dirt road. We passed under the overhead sign that announced we were not still in the real world but had just now entered the fantasy of the LAKEVIEW PARK midway, with its multi-colored tents, its promise of escape from reality, and the carousel.

But Jimmy had been right. The place was closed. Locked up, hiding all its wonderful secrets from the doubting eyes of an almost six-year-old.

"Don't worry," himself said. "You'll see."

About halfway to the park, my father turned to me. "Jocko," he said, "Do you know who might have used my razor blade to sharpen a pencil, say, maybe the day before yesterday?" Before I could answer, while I was still in the throes of indecision, he added, "No one is in trouble or anything. I would just like to ask that person to not do that again." I saw him shoot a humorous look across at me. "It was pretty dark when I shaved, and I spent the whole day with black lines down my face. Do you have any idea who might have done it?"

I knew this had to be a test. He had so many times told me, in no uncertain terms, that I was never to be a stool pigeon. He told me, "A man doesn't rat on his friends." So I knew that I certainly wasn't supposed to rat on my sister.

"I don't know, dad," I said. "Do you think it might have happened at the factory where they made the blades?"

He smiled. "I suppose that might be the case," he said.

"Maybe you should be real careful which ones you buy," I said.

"Don't push your luck, boyo." He smiled, and we dropped

the subject.

Other than us, there was only one person in the park when we walked up. He stood in his green work trousers and white T-shirt, smoking a cigarette outside the entrance to the carousel. As we approached, he snapped it onto the ground, stepped on it and walked forward to hesitantly shake hands with my father.

"You ready?" Dad asked him.

"Sure thing, Scrapper. A bet's a bet."

I never found out what they had bet on, but the payoff was that I would get the last ride on the Lakeview carousel before it was dismantled and shipped to the Netherlands. It was the very beginning of the decline of the amusement park that had fed the dreams of children and entertained adults for generations. Soon it would all be gone, but today I felt the strong hands of a shoe worker under my arms, and I was swept up onto the biggest white horse on the merry-go-round, with the gold trim and the real leather reins. The man in the green work pants threw the switch, and I was Li'l Beaver following Red Ryder on a wooden horse, saving the good people from the bad guys, enraptured in a world of calliope, fantasy, motion and the promise of a brass ring.

"Let me know when you're done," he shouted, and went outside to light another cigarette.

My old man had won at cards, or horses, or baseball, or something, and the payoff was to give me an experience I probably never would have gotten any other way, a solo ride on a perfect merry-go-round, accompanied by circus music, and I got to say when it was time to get off.

About an hour or two later, as we stood beside the cab in our own driveway, and my father was paying Jimmy, my mother came out the front door, and fantasy melted into reality.

"Jack, something has happened."

He looked at her face, furrowed his brow, patted Jimmy on the shoulder, turned and walked toward my mother. They walked together inside and sat at the kitchen table.

As I opened the screen door and entered the kitchen, I heard my mother say, "Jack, what did you do?"

"What? We went to Lakeview and…"

"Not that. Did you do something with the Flynns?"

"Oh, yeah. We brought in a union."

"Why?"

"The Portagees were getting stiffed. The shop was giving them a chit for every two cases of ladies' shoes. Then they even cut the rate. These guys couldn't feed their families on that. I mean, it was less than half of what some of us were getting. So we brought in a union."

"They fired you."

"They can't do that. I'm the union steward. The union won't stand for it."

"Well, they did stand for it. Sean and Casey were just here. Some deal was made. There isn't going to be any strike, any walkout, nothing. You got fired, and that's that."

"God damned no good lousy stinking sons of bitches! We were trying to help them."

But he didn't say "stinking."

"They have to feed their families," my mother reminded him.

"What about Sean and Casey?"

"They got fired too."

He looked down at his hand. It was maimed from the day the machine at work had malfunctioned and slammed through his finger and down into his foot. He had lost half his finger, and he had a scar on the top and bottom of his foot where the metal spike had gone through. He had gotten laid off, and I spent all day every day for a month or so attached to his pant leg because he couldn't work. He hadn't even asked the shop for money or sued them or anything. He just collected unemployment and waited to heal, and I got to learn how to talk like an unemployed and bitter shoe worker.

"I gave them everything, and that's what they do." He made a fist.

"Don't go to the bar?" my mother asked.

"No. I'll get a ride and go look for a job. There are plenty of other shoe shops around. I'll hitch on with one of them."

He walked off down the street to use the neighbors' phone to call a friend for a ride, and then he waited at the top of the driveway as if he were waiting for the school bus. I looked out the sun-porch window and watched him waiting. This man, this superman who was the best at basketball, the best at hitting birds with a rock, the best at attaching a sole to ladies shoes, the best looking, and obviously the best at making children, sat on the big rock at the end of the drive, his hands clasped behind his head, bent over at the waist. A black coupe pulled up, and he rose again to his feet and trotted around the back. He climbed into the front passenger seat.

When the car rolled off toward town, I turned from the window to see my mother behind me in the next room. She was looking at me. "Don't worry," she said. "It will be alright."

# CHAPTER 6
## The Creation and the Fall of Man

**IT WASN'T ALL RIGHT, THOUGH.** They had blackballed my father from all the shoe shops in town, and my family felt the sting of righteous hunger in a world dominated by want.

It was an October New Englanders dream about, and some pray for. A remnant of September warmth still clung to the yellowed hay fields. The call of the crows and the smell of burning leaves filled the neighborhood, but the nights were crisp and filled with the promise of the Headless Horseman or the Wolfman in the woods.

As I waited for the school bus, I collected a few leaves; one from a maple, one from an oak, and one from an elm. The maple was a bright red, the oak and elm yellow and green with orange outlines at the veins. It was a day we were all entrusted with bringing to school part of God's New England glory for display in our classrooms.

As we walked two-by-two into the classroom, Sister collected our bounty. She placed the pile on her desk for later use as adornments outlining the black board.

"One…"

I raised my hand, "Sister?"

"Yes, Mr. Hourihan?"

"Did God make all these leaves?"

She seemed eternally grateful for a religion question. "Yes, He did. Two…"

My hand shot up again. "Sister?"

"Yes?"

"Why didn't He just make them beautiful all the time? Why wait until October?"

She stood for a second or two, looking intently through her thin wire-framed glasses at me. Her expression reminded me of the one Seabee, my black and white Springer spaniel, would get when I would sit in front of him on a kitchen chair and explain things. First, she looked directly on, and then cocked her head to one side, and I could see her thinking.

"Three."

She continued to stare at me, since I was the last one to turn around and climb onto my chair. I had been expecting an answer.

"What is man, children?"

"Man is a creature compost of body and soul, and made to

the image and likeness of God, Sister."

I drifted off, intent on seeing Linda through our back door windows, but tuned back in at, "Who were the first man and woman?"

"The first man and woman were Adam and Eve, the first parents of the whole human race."

I was mired in the thought of the whole snake and apple thing and wondering why God would get so upset at people for eating a piece of fruit, but there it was, "Original Sin" and the whole human race got punished forever. Me too. And as I was wondering how I was to be punished, I heard the answer.

"What happened to Adam and Eve on account of their sin?"

"On account of their sin Adam and Eve lost sanctifying grace, the right to heaven, and their special gifts; they became subject to death, to suffering, and to a strong inclination to evil, and they were driven from the Garden of Paradise."

I understood what it felt like to be driven from paradise; someone had made me go to school. But at recess I sat on the black wrought-iron staircase that descended into the asphalt school yard from the second-floor rooms at St. Mary's. There were two of these staircases that descended from a single wrought iron grated platform at the second-floor back door. One went to the left, the other to the right. One was for boys. The other was for girls. I hunkered down a few steps from the bottom on the boys' side and watched the whole school population at play. My mother and father had played in this very school yard, and I wondered if they had done something then to get punished now. It seemed my father had done something good at the shop, and now we were all eating less meat and more dandelion greens, and the nights were getting colder without the aid of oil in the furnace. But if everyone on Earth could get punished for someone eating an apple at an inappropriate time, I guessed it wouldn't take much to get my old man fired from a shoe shop.

As I watched the school yard, I was looking to see if I could catch a glimpse of a "strong inclination to evil" in this chaos of innocence. I didn't want to think badly of my friends, but the instruction book said it was there, so it must be. Then in the midst of childhood purity I saw it. Mick and Tommy, two of my friends, were tormenting Marie; a French girl who was darker skinned than most of us Irishers. The Italians, by the luck of being even darker I supposed, went to a whole different school, the Sacred Heart School, a quarter mile down Main Street toward the Plains. Marie clutched her lunch bag in two arms and tried desperately to walk away from them, but they kept cutting her off, surrounding her like a demon posse.

"Cooties!" Tommy shouted as he reached out and touched her arm. Then both boys raced off to presumably give the cooties to someone else. The sea of children parted to let him through. No one wanted to be anointed with cooties.

Then Mick took another shot at collecting some cooties,

and the girl turned away. As she turned, she looked directly at me. I couldn't take the torment in her eyes as they filled up with tears. Without thinking, I found myself nearly transported to the scene of what was going on. I don't remember moving, but there I was standing between her and Tommy who was returning for more cooties.

"Get out of here!" I heard myself shouting. "Leave her alone, you God damn stupid bastard!"

Tommy stopped, but Mick started back toward us from the other side, and I shouted, "Mick so help me God, if you come over here again, I'm going to beat you within an inch of your stinking life." I didn't say "stinking" though. I had heard my father say that, and it seemed to work for him. It worked that day, too. As I stood there perched between this tormented girl and my friends, I wondered if this in fact wasn't the strong inclination to evil.

Everyone in our vicinity stood stock still and stared at what was happening. No one, it seemed, had ever stood up for Marie before. They all had just accepted that she must have cooties. It was good, because, as long as she was the target, that meant no one would accuse them of having cooties. Later, when the nun told my sisters how proud they should be of their little brother, and they came and told me, I wondered why the nuns hadn't done something themselves if they had seen it happen. It was a conundrum, since I knew all these kids had been in the same school, and all of them must have known right from wrong. I mean, that's what we were being taught, and my mother had said we were supposed to learn this stuff. I wondered if I too was inclined to evil.

On the bus ride home that afternoon, I wondered about what might have been evil in that day. I knew my language was supposed to be pretty bad, and I guess my friends were wrong to belittle a girl for no reason other than something they had made up, but I was sure that Marie being picked on every day, and no one standing up for her, not even the nuns, was probably the level of evil that the book was talking about.

I had just turned six on the Saturday before, and Danny Mac nearly choked to death on a peanut at my party. I became determined that day in the schoolyard to do as much good as I could. I wanted to be right clean of evil if I got a peanut caught in my throat and couldn't cough it up and died. That way I would go to heaven. Seemed like a good idea as I approached the age of reason, worried that my evil inclinations might someday arrive unannounced.

# CHAPTER 7
Keeping the Lord's Day Holy

**ON A SUNDAY, JUST BEFORE** All Souls' Day, we went to the eight o'clock Mass. The nuns took attendance so they would know who to punish on Monday in school. The eight o'clock Mass was the children's Mass. You could go to the others, but it was a venial sin. I loved the Mass. I loved the smell of incense, the drone of the priest speaking in Latin, the beauty of the statues and paintings and stained-glass windows, the flowers, the dust in the sunlight, and I could never understand why when Father Carbary said, "Go, the Mass is ended," everyone said in unison, "Thanks be to God." Were they all so happy that the Mass was over and they could leave?

Piously we filed out, up the main aisle, into the outer church, stopping only to anoint ourselves again with holy

## Baltimore Catechism: Clean Slate (Fall and Rise of a Catholic Boy)

water and the sign of the cross. I had been told the devil didn't like holy water, and this dipping your hand in and blessing yourself with it would drive the devil and any demons crazy. I didn't know about that, since I had seen some very bad men file through here, and never did I hear the devil in them complain about the dousing with holy water, so I wondered if it worked at all.

On this particular pilgrimage out of St. Mary's church, I was tucked between my mother and my sister Diane. When they both anointed themselves at the same time I got squeezed backwards, and then I just followed the crush of people out toward the door. It was just my luck that Sister Mary Patrick, the toughest nun God had ever made, was right there watching for just such heathen nonsense. She swooped in behind me and grabbed me by the collar. My mother and sister both looked back, but instead of protecting me from the holy banshee, they both laughed. Sister directed me back to the holy water fountain, and I got to bless myself before rejoining my waiting family.

We stepped out of the church and squinted into a bright, sunlit autumn morning. Some men had left after Holy Communion, walking directly from receiving the body and blood of Christ, straight up the center aisle, and out the doors so they could be the first to get their cars. Now they were parked in front of the church, waiting for the rest of their families to arrive.

One car caught my eye. It was a 1952 red Cadillac, parked

right in front of the church, ass end sticking out into the street. The guy in the black '40 Ford, blocked by the Caddy, laid on the horn.

My family stopped to buy the Sunday paper. The priest had given the Renard boys the coveted spot on the sidewalk directly in front of the church at the end of the front walkway to set up their wooden newspaper stand, and they were selling multicolored, funnies-covered Worcester Telegrams and Boston Globes as fast as they could hand them out and pocket thirty-five cents. When my mother had secured the day's news and tucked it under her arm we went, as we always did, to Grammy's house for a meal and family time. My mother would invariably get fifty cents back from Grammy since she would always keep the paper.

All seven of my father's siblings would bring their children, except Uncle Frankie who lived too far away and only showed up only occasionally with his family.

When I was done getting my Sunday clothes dirty climbing up the back of Grammy's barn, I scurried up the back stairs to the kitchen door following the heavy smell of baked ham. My father was already in trouble. He was being admonished by the matriarch of the family, his mother, Rose Anne Bridgette O'Flynn Hourihane herself, for his having been fired.

Grammy was a proud woman who had been born in County Meath to Briged Murry and John O'Flynn. It was the melding of a Catholic Irishman with a woman of "royal" background, her family having once run the Isle of Mann for the British. The Murrys descended from a noble Scotsman who fought the English in the north of Scotland while William Wallace fought them in the south, and when the fight was over the Murrys made peace with the Brits. John Murray, (He had added an "a" to the name, the same way the Hourihanes had dropped an "e.") Grammy's grandfather had been made the Governor in Chief of the Isle of Mann. By the time Rose came along, her mother and father had moved to County Meath on the Irish mainland. Grammy said she was born within sight of the Hill of Tara "where St. Patrick had lit his holy fire" to ease the transition from the old ways of the druids to the new ways of Christianity. In 1901, after a romantic tussle with a boy named Savage, her family shipped her off to America as an indentured servant to a rich family in New York. It was in the troubled streets of New York where she met the Irish Catholic Cornelius O'Hourihane, a self-professed member of the notorious Dead Rabbits gang. They got married and moved eventually to the Worcester diocese in Massachusetts. She had hoped her children would also become famous in the town of Milford. They sort of had, but in a different way from how she had expected. Anyway, that is what my cousin Sean told me.

"I suppose you're collecting unemployment now?" Grammy asked my father.

I stood just outside the doorway to the kitchen and watched. He sat with his elbows on the gray-speckled white

Formica table and his hands cradling a cup of coffee. She towered over him, leaning both hands on the chair back directly across the table from him. Her hair was in a gray bun, her print dress and apron were made out of the same material, and her glasses had dropped down on her nose as if they were afraid if they hadn't they would melt from the intensity of her stare. He just sat at the kitchen table looking into his cup of coffee. He appeared to me as I must have appeared to him on days when I locked onto my uneaten supper while he told me to eat my squash or I would "damn sure be eatin' it for breakfast."

"Unemployment," she muttered it as if it were a curse word, "and what d'ya suppose everyone is saying about ya now? Seven kids and no job. Shame on ya!"

He rose from the table, walked to the sink, poured out the rest of his coffee, rinsed the cup dutifully, and left it in the sink, then turned back to his mother. No one talked back to Grammy. Even the priests and nuns seemed afraid of her.

"At least I don't have to move to Holyoke," he said meaningfully. He stood his ground and stared at his mother, knowing he was no longer her favorite, as he had been growing up. She wiped her hands on her apron and turned back toward the oven to tend the ham that needed basting.

As I did when I wanted truth, I went to Sean, who was older by several years. We sat on the back steps, and I asked him, "What'd he mean, move to Holyoke?"

"Uncle Frankie," Sean said with a knowing grin. Sean was

eleven years old, but he was the size of a sixteen-year-old, and he seemed to know more about our family than any of the other cousins. "He had to move to Holyoke when he got out of the Air Force. See, he got in a fight at the Pond Bar with a guy who called him an IRA baby-killer, and the guy he hit fell down and hit his head on a rock and died, so Chief Mac comes to the house and tells Grammy that Uncle Frankie has to get out of town, because he has to come arrest him in the morning for murder. So, Frankie up and moves to Holyoke, and the whole thing is somehow forgotten. Stuff was different back then, but I think that's what Uncle Jack meant."

I was stunned. The only murder I had ever heard of before this was Cain and Abel. Uncle Frankie was the nicest of all my uncles and would never hurt anyone on purpose. Wow, so I guessed unemployment, hunger, and a slip in the social structure were a much better deal.

Shortly after this revelation, I learned about sin. It seemed to be perfect timing, just when I was beginning to figure my whole family, except Grammy and my mother, was "headed for hell in a hand basket." The rules I learned that week, the ones associated with sin, seemed to let at least some of my family off the hook.

On the school bus ride the next morning, I sat with Linda. We didn't talk much anymore. We were still trying to figure out why she wasn't allowed to play in the woods, and why we had to be put on different sides of the playground at school, boys' side; girls' side. And why boys and girls were separated in class, boys' side, girls' side. And although we spent summers together on her swings, under the watchful eye of her mother who periodically peeked out the second story kitchen window, we didn't talk anymore on the bus ride. It was sort of a confusing embarrassment.

That day, I reached over as I got up from the seat and touched her hand, just to let her know I was still the same person, and she was still my best friend. Then I hurried down the aisle of the bus, down the two steps and into the front school yard. Linda and I never touched again.

Within a few minutes the bell rang, and we all fell into lines of two-by-two, girls holding hands with girls, boys with boys. A John Philip Sousa march began to play; you know the one, "Be kind to your web-footed friends, cause that duck might be somebody's mother." My cousin Sean had told me the words.

We all started into the school, fingers on our lips to remind ourselves not to talk. There was a "no talking in line" rule, and I believed that it must be a sin, so I was pretty good about this except to occasionally make a noise like cymbals in the pauses of the march. It just seemed it should be there.

"One."

Books slammed shut, and we muffled to a standing position.

"Two."

Rubber soles squeaked as they spun around on hardwood

floors to face the back of the room.

"Three."

I clasped my hands in prayer and turned my head to the left to peer into the next room.

It seemed from last night's lessons that there were three types of sin. There was the "Original" one that I didn't do and couldn't do a thing about. I didn't cause it, and I was told that Jesus and Baptism made it go away, so I ignored it.

According to the pictures in our book, there were venial sins and mortal sins.

Venial sin was when our perfectly white bottle of milk, which started out pure as a clean slate, got some black spots in it. Then when we did a mortal sin it got all black, and, as Fitzy, the kid who sat in front of me, said, it became chocolate milk. This seemed confusing since we all liked chocolate milk a lot more than white, but since it cost more, only the rich kids got chocolate milk. I seldom got any, except when Sister plunked one on my desk "by mistake." Later, I learned that when someone was absent who had already paid for milk, Sister gave it to me. Today, as I knelt on my chair thinking forward to Halloween and ungodly amounts of candy, Sister's voice broke in.

"What three things are necessary to make a sin mortal, children?"

"To make a sin mortal, these three things are needed, Sister: The thought, desire, word, action, or omission must be seriously wrong or considered seriously wrong; the sinner, must be mindful of the serious wrong; the sinner must fully consent to it."

It occurred to me that my Uncle Frankie didn't fully consent to killing that guy. From what I heard, the guy kept calling him an "IRA baby-killer," and he just wanted to shut the loud mouth up, so it couldn't have been a mortal sin. He was just defending his Irish Catholic honor.

"What is venial sin, children?"

"Venial sin is a less serious offense against the law of God, which does not deprive the soul of sanctifying grace, and which can be pardoned even without sacramental confession, Sister."

I guessed they pardoned Uncle Frankie. So, I figured he didn't get arrested because what he did was a mistake, and he didn't give his full consent to the big mouth dying. It was an accident, so I guess it was a venial sin at worst, and he was saved, and the talking in line thing wasn't a sin at all, so I was okay, too.

## All Souls Day

According to Cousin Sean, All Souls Day was "just another name for Halloween."

I was, therefore, pretty surprised when Sister told us that All Souls Day was to be on Sunday, two days after Halloween. She stood in front of the room. Her eyes glassed over as she explained the importance of the day, which was about a place called Purgatory. It had to do with dead relatives and other people who, "have not been cleansed from the temporal punishment due to venial sins and from attachment to mortal sins and cannot immediately attain the beatific vision in heaven."

So they weren't hell bound but weren't ready for heaven. I got that. And prayer could help them, so this was the day when you prayed for them, but there was still something important I didn't understand, so I raised my hand.

"Sister, since Halloween is on Friday, and All Souls Day is on Sunday do we get to go out for candy both days?" My classmates laughed, but not too loudly, only what they couldn't stifle.

"Mr. Hourihan. Halloween and All Souls Day are two distinctly different days, and if you are poking fun at a holy day of our church woe betide you. You will end up in the Britannica."

I didn't wait to be called on. I didn't even raise my hand. "What?" I couldn't help myself. "What's the Britannica?"

"It is a big box. You will be put in it and be sent to China, and you will never see your mother and father again. Do you understand?"

Whoa. I didn't see that one in *The Baltimore Catechism*. I guess that poking fun at things was even worse than a mortal sin. I looked at Jake, and he shrugged. His frightened wide eyes said he hadn't heard of it either.

I promised myself I would never poke fun at All Souls Day, but that didn't stop the nightmares.

"Yes, Sister." I cowered.

We learned about how the Holy Ghost gave us superpowers. I didn't understand that, but that's what it said in the book. I was not about to poke fun at it, or I would find myself in the middle of the night again trying to claw my way out of the box, and then when I did get it open, finding myself floating in the middle of an endless ocean presumably on my way to China and scared shitless.

On the eve before All Saints' Day (the night before the day before All Souls' Day) I stood motionless in the kitchen, my arms outstretched like Christ on the cross, while my sister Diane finished outfitting me with my Halloween costume. She had taken an old sheet from the dresser, cut holes in it for the eyes and mouth, crimped it together under the arms with safety pins, and tightened it at the waste with one of her own white belts. Since there were holes in the sheet, well, you guessed it. I went trick or treating as the Holy Ghost. What Sister didn't know couldn't land me in the Britannica, I guessed. So, with the promise to pray on Sunday for the souls in Purgatory, I went out with my sisters to collect as much candy as I could before my father would come find us and drag us home.

# CHAPTER 8
## The Virtues and Gifts of the Holy Ghost

HALLOWEEN WAS WONDERFUL, BAGS FULL of Three Musketeers and Necco Wafers, Mary Janes, and Bonomo's Turkish Taffy, walking through the neighborhood scaring people, and a cup of warm apple cider and cookies at the VanHorfs', Linda's grandparents who lived in the same house but downstairs. Then I had a fitful night's sleep. I dreamed of things blowing up all around me. I put my head under my coat, and I woke to a Saturday afternoon hockey game on the radio. The next day was All Souls' Day, and I fulfilled my promise of prayer for the people in Purgatory, and then came Monday.

The bus was a continuous smile from seat to seat, since we

all had candy in our brown paper lunch bags or Roy Rogers and Dale Evans lunch boxes. That was always confusing to me. How could they have different last names if they were married? It made no Catholic sense.

"Three."

"What are the chief supernatural powers that are bestowed on our souls with sanctifying grace?"

Since the non-readers all were learning these lessons based on what people told them, there were often strange and unexplainable mistakes in their answers.

"The chief supernatural powers that a beast stowed on our souls with sanctifying grace are the mumble mumble three mumble virtues and the seven gifts of the Holy Ghost, Sister."

"We'll come back to that one, children."

I snuck a look back at Sister, and she was smiling a big wide smile that seemed to hint that she knew how difficult it might be to study while eating more candy in one night than we would have for the rest of the year, except possibly at Easter. Easter made no Catholic sense to me at all. "On the third day, He arose again from the dead and ate a bunch of candy?" I never understood it.

"What are the three theological virtues?"

After an unintelligible attempt, the good sister, making her "this was a very important part," face, stopped us and read the answer. "The three theological virtues are faith, hope, and charity. And the greatest of these is charity."

From the way I saw it after the lesson, faith was that we

believed in what we are told about the religion even if we don't see any proof, we have hope that God will keep his promises, and charity means we should love God and take care of others if we can.

I got stuck on the faith thing, so I raised my hand after lunch and asked, "Sister, if faith is believing in something even if we don't know it's true, how is that different from being just plain ignorant?"

Now, I had heard this argument at Grammy's house one Sunday from Uncle Normand (my uncle by virtue of his marriage to my sainted Aunt Pamela.) He came late, and then he and my Uncle Con got into it about religion, so I thought it would be an excellent one to bring up here. It wasn't.

"Mr. Hourihan, that is blasphemy."

Uncle Con had called it "drunken nonsense."

"Now, there's a new word," I thought. It sounded as if this "blasphemy" was a very bad thing. I guessed Uncle Normand was going to hell in a hand basket.

"Yes, Sister." I couldn't think of anything else to say.

"One."

My stomach was grumbling because one of my sisters had made my lunch, and when I opened the bag, I found a note, a hard-boiled egg, and two slices of bread. The note said, "Make it yourself, you little brat." I think it had to do with the holes I cut in someone's kerchief, figuring it would be nice if she had a place for her ears to stick out. My fashion design wasn't appreciated, I guess.

"Two."

I really had to pee.

"Three."

As I marveled that "three" rhymed with "pee," I knelt up tall on my chair, tightened my knees a little and got ready for our questions.

"Which are the seven gifts of the Holy Ghost, children?"

"The seven gifts of the Holy Ghost are: wisdom, understanding, counsel, fortitude, knowledge, piety, and fear of the Lord."

I didn't know what any of those super powers meant, so I chalked it up to faith. Truth be told though, the fear I had was not of God but of the nun standing in the front of the room with a wooden pointer and her eyes burning a hole in the back of my head.

"Which are the twelve fruits of the Holy Ghost?"

"The twelve fruits of the Holy Ghost are: charity, joy, peace, patience, benignity, goodness, long-suffering, mildness, faith, modesty, continence, and chastity."

"And apples, I think." I hadn't intended to say it as loudly as I had. It was meant only for Jake, who was my best friend in school and knelt right across from me, but I had underestimated the power of a soft voice in the midst of total silence. I winced and waited for the pointer.

Nothing happened for a few seconds, and I thought, "Again, faith." I accepted the twelve fruits, but the only one

I asked anyone about was continence, and my aunt told me it was when you kept yourself from peeing when you really had to go. Incontinence, she said, was the opposite, and she laughed, but not hard.

"Recite the eight beatitudes, children."

The following was a cacophony of mumbled piety. Sure we all got the "Blessed are the" but the rest jumbled into a mess of "I hope she doesn't realize I don't know the words."

This is how I remembered it, and recited it for my mother later that day she laughed and said, "Perfect. Go get an apple."

"Blessed are the poor and spirits, for theirs is the kingdom of heaven.

Blessed are the meat, for they shall possess the earth.

Blessed are they who moon, for they shall control the comforted.

Blessed are they who hunger and thirst, mumble-mumble sake, for they shall pee satisfied.

Blessed are the merciful, for they shall obtain mercy. (That was the easy one, so we all regrouped here, took a breath, and pushed on.)

Blessed are the clean apart, for they shall seek God.

Blessed are the pieceworkers, for they shall be called children of God. (My father helped me with that one.)

Blessed are they who suffer persecution for justice's sake, for theirs is the kingdom of heaven, or they get fired and blackballed..." (My father, again.)

"Okay, we'll work on that one, children. Are there any

other virtues besides the theological virtues of faith, hope, and charity?"

Stunned silence.

"Okay, children, we'll move on."

# CHAPTER 9
## The Catholic Church

**AND MOVE ON WE DID.** We had come so far from "Who made us? God made us," and the good sister must have known, as I did, that the questions and answers in the book were getting too long for us to memorize, so one day she took a different approach. As she opened her mouth to speak that morning, everyone instinctively began to rise.

"No, no, no, children." She got up from behind her desk, walked around to the front, and leaned back against it.

"Today we'll try something different. Let's just talk, okay?"

Some mumbled, "Okay, Sister," as if we had actually been asked for our permission. Sister smiled at the response.

"I suppose you all know that the church is the building where we go every Sunday and Holy Day of Obligation. But when we say, 'the church,' we mean more.

"The Church our Lord Jesus Christ founded to bring us eternal salvation is the congregation of all baptized persons united in the same true faith, the same sacrifice, and the same sacraments, under the authority of the Sovereign Pontiff and the bishops in communion with him.

"Did you know that?" she asked.

How could we know that? No one answered. We were all about six years old; truth be told, we didn't *know* anything.

"The church is the dwelling of the Holy Ghost." She looked around at the blank faces then added, "The first time the Holy Ghost was seen was on Pentecost Sunday, when He came down upon the apostles in the form of tongues of fire."

All right, now I was interested. Tongues of fire!? I turned and wagged my tongue at Jake, but didn't get caught.

"Let me read you something," she said, and opened a book. "And when the days of Pentecost were drawing to a close, they were all together in one place. They being the apostles, of course. And suddenly there came a sound from heaven, as of a violent wind blowing, and it filled the whole house where they were sitting. And there appeared to them parted tongues as of fire, which settled upon each of them. And they were all filled with the Holy Ghost and began to speak in foreign tongues, even as the Holy Ghost prompted them to speak."

"Holy shit," I thought and looked at Jake. His brown eyes widened, his wide shoulders shrugged, and he shook his head.

Then he opened his mouth wide and wagged his tongue at me. A devil in a Saturday morning cartoon had done this once, and we had picked it up.

The vision of tongues of fire, sounds of heaven, wind blowing, and foreign languages filled my mind for the rest of the day. I went to Jake's house after school to play and maybe sneak down to Fino Field to run the bases. As we entered the mud room at his home, the softest words I didn't understand came from the adjoining kitchen.

"Jacques, c'est toi?"

"Yeah, it's me, Ma."

I looked through the doorway and saw his mother sitting at an ironing board with three baskets of clean clothes at her feet.

I had seen her before, at Mass with her family. I would look for them each Sunday since we children were instructed to leave our parents and go to the front rows of pews and sit together. It gave the nuns a better view of who was present and, more importantly, who wasn't. Jake would always sit with me. His brothers sat with their own grade. His oldest brother Henry, who, at sixteen, had gone to the shoe shop, would sit with their mother in the back.

The voice came from the kitchen again.

"Et c'est qui?"

Jake went directly to the refrigerator, opened it, and stuck his head inside. "It's John Hourihan, Ma, from school."

"Hourihan? Votre mere est Genevieve?"

I knew the name was my mother's even though Mrs. Dubois pronounced it John-vee-ev instead of Jen-a-veeve.

"Yes ma'am, she's my mother."

"Vous etes intelligent, comme elle est?"

"Yeah, ma, he's smart," Jake answered for me.

My friend was in a hurry to get back outside after grabbing a couple pancakes from the fridge, but I was hypnotized.

Some of my own ancestors and family members spoke with a brogue, but they spoke English, and the only other language I had heard was the universal Catholic language of Latin, which wasn't a real language because no one except the priests and nuns and a few high school students actually spoke it. But here was a woman washing other people's clothes for enough money to feed her six children, and she was speaking in a foreign language. And Jake understood it.

I searched the room for a tongue of fire, convinced that only the Holy Ghost could make this happen.

I stepped into the kitchen, stunned. I scanned the upper reaches of the room and found nothing.

She turned and looked inquiringly at me. She was a little woman, smaller than my mother, and with black hair pulled tightly back in a net. She was beautiful with deep brown eyes. Jake, with his curly black hair, broad shoulders, round face, and dark skin must have taken after his father.

After a few moments of silence, I asked, "Do you know the Holy Ghost?"

"Le Saint-Esprit?" She squinted her eyes for a few seconds

then called, "Jacques?"

He came back into the room eating a cold pancake, handed one to me, and stood beside me.

She spoke again so Jake could translate.

"Le Saint-Esprit est la verite."

"She says the Holy Ghost is truth."

She waited for a few seconds and continued, "Et la verite est si je ne termine pas cette central vapeur nous ne mangent pas." She smiled and turned back around to the ironing board.

"Why do you wash and iron other people's clothes?" I asked.

She understood, probably because I was staring at the baskets of clothes at her feet.

"Parce que je suis pauvre."

I looked to Jake.

"Because we're poor."

He turned to go, but I wasn't done. "My father says poverty is a sin."

"Poverty is not… Pauvrete n'est pas un peche… n'est pas un vice. Ton pè devrait savoir." She looked at her son, waited for a few seconds then spit out "Dites-lui!"

He finished his pancake and said, "I don't think she likes your father."

"Why not?"

"I don't know. Is he French?"

"No, he's Irish."

"Maybe that's it. Let's go." He led the way outside, but

as we left I heard her say, "Dites bonjour à votre mère de la parte d'Yvonne."

As we stepped out onto the back porch I heard again, "Dites-lui!"

Jake said, "She says to say hello to your mother. I think she likes her."

Maybe it was because they were both French.

## The Power to Teach

The next day, religion class went on right up until lunch. We learned all about the Holy Ghost, tongues of fire, and about how the church would teach us the "one true religion." I loved this church. It was like having a second mother, the way it protected us and taught us how to live. And then, after we returned from the schoolyard, religion class began again. This was not normal, but I didn't mind missing the times tables and how the Christians rescued our country from the hands of the godless Indians. Of course, that second part, the history of the Indians being godless enemies, did nothing to explain Tonto, Li'l Beaver or Straight Arrow, three of my childhood heroes.

By the time I had tucked my lunch bag into my lift-top desk, looked for Linda through the window of the back door, and turned back to the front of the room, Sister was already teaching.

"Christ gave the power to teach, to sanctify, and to rule the members of His Church to the apostles, the first bishops of the Church and their successors. The priests, especially parish priests, assist the bishops in the care of souls."

I couldn't help it. I had never heard Sister make such a glaring error. Before I could even raise my hand, it just came out.

"And the sisters."

Everyone in the class turned in horror that I had spoken without permission.

"Do you have something to add, Mr. Hourihan?"

"The power to teach, Sister. You have that too, right?"

She kept her hand on the page but gently closed the book. She squinted her eyes for what seemed a long time. She must have decided I was asking in earnest and responded.

"Yes, we Sisters of Saint Joseph have permission to teach. We are a teaching order, by permission of the bishop. It is our mission."

"Do you get to teach more when you become priests?"

"Nuns can't be priests," she said with the kind of subservient smile that my mother sometimes used when she disagreed with what she was about to say.

She waited for me to nod my understanding. I nodded, even though I understood nothing.

"And, children, you have a right to teach, also." She returned to her page, "The laity of the Church are all its members who do not belong to the clerical or to the religious state. The laity can help the Church in her care of souls by leading lives that will reflect credit on the Church, and by cooperating with their bishops and priests, especially through Catholic Action.

"The laity can participate actively in the apostolate of the Church when they arouse the interest of non-Catholics in the Catholic faith."

It made no sense, and soon we moved on to history class and the first Thanksgiving. We drew pictures of turkeys, Pilgrims, fish, Indians, and corn plants, to be taped to the windows of the school. We learned the words papoose, squaw, brave, scalp, guns, missionaries and treaties, and then we moved on to the settling of our New World.

# CHAPTER 10
Arousing the Interest

**IT WAS THE END OF** autumn, and with the holidays coming, my mother again took on a job at the hat shop. Since she "had a bun in the oven" they let her work from home this time. No one back then said the word "pregnant." It was a bun in the oven, on the nest, or in a family way, but not pregnant. That was a forbidden word. It was probably a venial sin or something.

With six kids, and my father spending part of his unemployment check at Tibby's Bar, Mom was preparing for a string of the most expensive holidays of the year. First there was the day of giving thanks for the unexpected charity of the godless Indians. That was followed by the celebration of the virgin birth of Jesus, and then came New Year's, which wasn't religious but cost money anyway. I didn't know we would soon also be celebrating the birth of Cornelius Joseph the second, to be named after my grandfather. One day my father came home from work early in a taxi, my mother met him in the front yard, and they were whisked off. My cousin Joan, who was nineteen and married, came to babysit us. A few days later, Mom came home with my new brother. Not much changed, except for the noise.

On the Saturday before Thanksgiving, I sat on the front porch steps and waited. Today was the day Buster would bring my mother's homework to the house and pick up the ladies' hats she had finished during the week. As the white cube truck of the Lish Hat Company turned off Purchase Street into our long dirt driveway, I stood, turned, and pushing open the screen door I leaned inside and announced, "He's here."

The arrival of Buster was, for me, a holiday in itself. It always went like this: after he picked up the several boxes of finished hats and dropped off the new ones to be assembled, I got to sit with him on the bumper of the truck, split a soda, and talk baseball. My mother would save an orange soda for Buster. It was his favorite. She liked him because he had been good to her when she had worked at the hat shop, and, since

Saturday was also grocery shopping day, he sometimes gave us a ride to town to save us the taxi fare. My father liked him because, as he told me, "He's a good man who works hard, pays what he owes, and provides for his family." There wasn't much else that my old man respected more. I guess it was because he knew how hard that was for an Irishman to do, and how especially hard it was for a negro, like Buster.

"How ya doin, Johnny?" the big man said as he used the box he was carrying to push inside the front door I was still holding open.

"Okay," I said, following him inside.

"In the corner, right over there," my mother said, pointing to an empty corner of the kitchen.

Buster placed the box on the floor and returned to the truck for the second one.

"Where are the finished ones, Gen?" he asked.

"They're in the den, near the TV."

As Buster went to get the boxes, my mother went to the ice box and took a Miscoe orange soda from the case, and I followed him into the next room. He looked curiously at the rhinestones that were supposed to be adorning the women's hats my mother had crafted, but which were all over the floor. He looked at me and squinted his eyes. I told him how my mother had gone to a neighbor's last night, and upon leaving she had told me in no uncertain terms, "I don't want to see these rhinestones all over the place when I get back." While she was gone, I had convinced Dennis to play catch with them a handful at a time. We played, we laughed, we didn't catch many, and then, just before my mother had returned, I had turned out the lights so she wouldn't see them. She had said she didn't want to see them. She didn't say we couldn't play. I had spent the next few hours, under her watchful eyes, trying to pick them all up, but I had been run off to bed before I got to all of them. He laughed. "I'm still in trouble," I said. He laughed harder while carrying the boxes out of the house.

I never knew Buster's last name. My father told me it was because some guy named Jim Crow said he didn't have one. I figured he did have a last name but didn't want to piss off this Crow guy, who must have been really big since Buster himself was bigger than my father.

Buster placed the boxes in the truck and came back to the front door where my mother waited and handed him the soda. That was the cue for me to go sit on the bumper of the truck. Buster would shake hands with my mother and then come sit with me, leaning back against the warmth of the truck's back door.

The first time this happened, Buster had turned to her, nodded at me on his bumper, and asked, "You mind if we share this?"

"It's your soda. I believe you get to choose who you want to share it with." They both laughed, and he came and sat beside me. It became a ritual: he arrived, I held the door, Mom got the soda, we sat on the bumper and drank it. Today I had a new kind of question for him; for a change, it wasn't about baseball.

"Buster, do you think us Catholics should try to find non-Catholics and," I searched for the words I had learned. "interest them in the Catholic faith?"

He looked down at me and smiled. Slowly he said, "I don't know for sure, little man. I'm not a Catholic."

My mouth dropped open, and I turned more toward my adult friend.

"Why not?" I asked in shock. I couldn't understand why a good person like Buster would be anything but a Catholic. Catholic being the only one true religion, and Catholics being the only people who could go to heaven.

"Well, because… here have some soda." He leaned his head back against the truck door and closed his eyes for a few seconds while I drank. "I guess because my parents were Baptists."

"Like John the Baptist?"

"Right." He took the soda back and swigged.

"But he was a Catholic I think."

"I think you should talk to your parents about this."

Buster handed me the rest of his orange soda, tussled my hair, and walked me away from the truck to the back door.

"So, the only difference you see between you and me is that I'm not a Catholic?"

"I guess." For a moment I wondered whether or not I should mention the obvious. I mean, there was another difference that anyone could see. I decided I should mention it, or at least it would be okay if I did. I looked up at him and said, "And, well, you're a grown-up."

He patted my shoulder as he turned and headed back to the truck. "You're a good boy." He jumped into the cab of the truck. "See you next time," he said and drove off laughing.

I was confused. Later, while I was practicing throwing stones at the sign in the barn, it occurred to me that Buster was the first non-Catholic I had ever met, and *The Baltimore Catechism* said I should try to interest him in the Catholic faith, or he'd be going to hell, but my parents said he was a good man, and it seemed unfair to me that Buster wouldn't be going to heaven just because he was a Baptist.

Before the truck was out of sight my eyes watered, and I prayed to God that there was orange soda in hell.

# CHAPTER 11
The Resurrection and Life Everlasting

**THANKSGIVING WAS FULLY ON OUR** minds as we returned to school that Monday. I dutifully followed the line of children up the cold granite steps into the building, two-by-two, fingers to our lips for silence, and sat down in my back-row seat. I was still concerned with the plight of Buster. I was determined to pray for his soul and his eventual entry into heaven. What I was going to learn today was probably going to accomplish that, even without my prayers. You see, there were a lot of contradictions in the Catholic faith, and when one lesson contradicted another, we Catholics tended to just believe the one we liked. It was sort of like religion by multiple choice.

But before the few days off for Thanksgiving, we had to run

through a ritual that we had been taught weeks ago.

"Duck and cover!" Sister nearly shouted suddenly, and the room turned upside down as thirty-two children slid from their chairs, filed row by row into the hallway where the coats were hanging on a line of hooks on the wall. We each found our own coat, squatted down, and then stood up with our heads under them. We were told it would protect us during an atomic bomb blast. It was the alternative to hiding under our desks. When we returned to our seats fully confident that we had survived the attack from the godless communist Russians and sat back down, Sister sat in silence with her hands folded in front of her as if in prayer. Slowly she stood and walked to the front of her desk.

"Children, I have some terrible news."

This had never happened before. For the most part, bad news—such as the fact that our coats would not keep us alive during an atomic blast—was hidden from us children, a sort of white lie. White being good, black being bad, as evidenced in our milk bottles of sin.

"A third grader, Paul Anderson, has succumbed to polio."

Although we all knew what polio was, I had no idea what "succumbed" meant, but then Sister went the extra step.

"He died last night at Milford Hospital."

The news was devastating to first-graders. Death was a mystery that happened far away in distance or in age, but for a boy we all knew, who was only in the third grade, in a room just down the hall, to die, to just end, was frightening.

"One." We stood in silence.

"Two." We turned.

"Three." There was whimpering and sniffling behind me, so I refused to turn around to see who it was.

"Today, children, we will say a good Act of Contrition."

This set the rest of the class off into an undercurrent of sobbing. We knew the prayer wasn't for Paul. If you are dead, an Act of Contrition is too late. This was for us. The nun was getting us ready just in case it was our turn next. She wanted us to be in a state of grace and ready for heaven, which is what a good Act of Contrition would do. It scared the hell out of me.

After the prayer, she appropriately turned to *The Baltimore Catechism* and read, "I believe in... the resurrection of the body and life everlasting."

It was nice to hear that, with the threats of atomic war and polio, we would all be risen from the dead and allowed to live forever. I wondered, if it happened, would I have to go back to the first grade or could I go back to my paradise on Purchase Street. We learned some wonderful and terrifying things in 1952 at St. Mary's; things that gave us hope and things that would frighten us for the rest of our lives.

Sister was once again teaching our lessons.

"By the resurrection of the body is meant that at the end of the world the bodies of all men will rise from the earth and be united again to their souls, nevermore to be separated."

My hand shot up.

As if exhausted from a hard day's work, she stopped reading. "Yes, Mr. Hourihan?"

"Sister, does that mean Baptists too?"

"The good will be rewarded, and the damned will be punished."

So Buster would go to heaven after all. I thought that was only fair.

"Good for God," I said earnestly.

"Mr. Hourihan, go stand in the corner and face the wall."

"Yes, Sister," I said happily.

My mother had explained this to me the last time it had happened. She said I was overly energetic, and when Sister did this, it was to help me concentrate on what was being said. Myself, I thought in terms of baseball. It made things clearer. So as the good sister spoke of "immediate" and "general" judgment, I supposed that heaven was like being at bat, and hell was being in the field, and purgatory was sitting on the bench waiting to play. Then, at the end of the game when all the runs were counted, the winners were declared. It made more sense to me that way. Later in the year, when I learned about limbo, I supposed that was like the junior little league where you get to use the equipment, but you don't really play the game. If you died with a mortal sin on your soul you were sent to hell, venial sin sent you to purgatory, and a state of grace sent you to heaven. This was all making so much sense now. I loved this religion.

## CHAPTER 12
Resurrection Hits Home

**WE HAD A HALF-DAY** of school on Wednesday, and it was a good thing we did.

When the big yellow bus carted us home from St. Mary's, it hissed and whined to a stop at the top of the quarter-mile driveway to the house. There was a big black Plymouth parked down in front of the house. It belonged to one of the Flynn boys. I had seen it before when they had picked my father up for work, back when they all had a job. By the time we had reached halfway to the house, my father was standing outside the car and waving for us to hurry up.

"C'mon," he shouted. "I need some help. Get the lead out. Run like the divil is chasing ya."

Nancy, Sheila, and I began to run. Patty and Diane didn't run for anyone. They were too grown up, Diane at 10 and

Patricia at 11, and they had fully learned a fierce Irish independence the rest of us would eventually assimilate. As I arrived at the car, I glanced in through the open door of the big back seat and saw bag after brown paper bag of groceries. I had never seen so many bags of food in one place. I looked back at my father in confusion.

"Start haulin' them in," he said with a smile.

My three-year-old brother Dennis, who was extremely strong for a kid, was already toddling into the house carrying a five-pound red net of potatoes. The bags filled the kitchen table top, and then we stacked some on the floor in front of it. My father thanked Casey and said goodbye. Casey glanced into the back seat in confusion at the remaining bags.

"Those are yours," my father said.

They smiled and shook hands, and he returned to the kitchen.

He looked down at me for a second, sensed my confusion, and said, "I got a job."

I went immediately to the refrigerator (My father called it the ice box). I grabbed up all the dandelion greens that were limply nestled in the crisper drawer, took them outside without a word and threw them on top of the manure pile. I wouldn't be eating any more of those vile bitter weeds for a while. I returned and grabbed the two winter squashes.

"Not the squash," my mother said with a smile. "You'll be eating the squash."

My father patted me on the back and laughed. "Nice try."

The prize of the grocery haul was a 26-pound turkey. It was the biggest bird I had ever seen, and I wondered how it had ever gotten off the ground. While I was unloading and putting away the groceries, I managed to pocket one of the three cans of crabmeat. I had ideas for it.

This was to be a great Thanksgiving for us. Although somewhere halfway through a huge drumstick, I wondered how Paul Anderson's family was feeling on this day of thanks. Although I was still too young for my first Holy Communion, having not reached the age of reason, I did understand already that we were all supposed to care about the trials of other people, like the Portagese at the shoe shop. But this was Thanksgiving, and boy did we eat! It was as if I had opened my mouth like the opening of the Hoover Dam, and the food flowed through like water. After the dishes had been washed and dried and put away, we all listened again to my father tell us about his new job.

"So, I walked in the front door of Bickford Shoe, down there on Depot Street, big as life, and they all knew who I was. So, Biff, who works there as a sidelaster, nods toward the office door. I knocked on the door and didn't even wait for an answer, just opened it up and walked in, and I said, 'I'm here for a job. I'm Jack Hourihan, and I'm the best bedlaster this side of the Atlantic.'

"Then this little guy, all dressed to the nines with a suit and tie, says for me to sit down. So I sit down, and he says he knows who I am and why I'm there. Then, by God, the son-of-a-bitch says 'You got the job.' Just like that. He says he started out piss-poor and has a lot of kids too, and then he says, 'Jack, I know what it's like to be Irish. I'm a Jew. They don't like us either. Go have Thanksgiving. Come in Monday.' Then he gives me a few bucks in advance to buy what we need."

We all slept fine on Thanksgiving night. It was as if my family breathed a combined sigh of relief. We had turned another corner in a long and corner-filled road.

# PART II
# The Commandments

## CHAPTER 13
The Two Great Commandments

IT WAS A WEEK AFTER Thanksgiving, and we were back to normal before the run-up to Christmas. The girls were told over breakfast what they would be doing for Saturday. Diane was assigned to the laundry; Patty, the ironing; Nancy was nominated to wash the kitchen floor, and Sheila was to "watch the kids," a job that had just increased incredibly with Neil in the carriage needing to be fed, changed, and protected from bees.

I was one of "the kids" for a few more years, and therefore, rather than doing a chore, I *was* a chore, like washing the clothes and hanging them on the line. Sitting in the unseasonable warmth of the late fall sun, in the dirt between the back door and the barn, how could I possibly know how close death was about to come to us?

My sister had become tired of dressing her dolls and decided I was a favorable alternative. I protested, but she was in charge, so there I sat on a bench, a seven-foot long, one-by-six plank placed across two cement blocks under which snakes sometimes hid, just outside the back door, in the warm sun, in a green and yellow sun dress.

Suddenly a crunch of gravel in the driveway brought Sheila to her feet. She slowly ambled the fifteen or so feet to the corner of the house and peeked around into the driveway.

"You stay there!" she said in her almost authoritative voice, and she ran off to see what the Cushman Bakery truck driver would bring into the house.

I walked to the front of the house and sat on the back bumper of the truck as I always did when Buster brought hats in the Lish Hat shop truck, and I waited for her to return. Suddenly, the black and white panel truck lurched and jumped and started up the drive. I was dumped off the bumper, but the hem of the dress hooked around a trailer hitch at the back. The hem looped the silver ball and then tore a hole between the dress and the hem and kept me fastened tightly to the moving truck. When the driver reached the end of the driveway he stopped, and I began to stand and reach to untangle myself. Before I could free myself, the truck was moving again. I fell to my knees. He turned right, and I was dragged along the asphalt expanse of Purchase Street. As he picked up speed, the dress pulled tighter. I felt like those cowboys who get dragged behind a horse through the town by the bad guys. It had the same effect. As we approached Linda's house, about a quarter-mile up the road, Linda's grandmother ran to the street shouting at the driver to stop.

He wasn't seeing her, so I reached up as far as I could and grabbed the silver ball. With my right hand I pulled myself up to the truck, still dragging on my knees on the road, and I unhooked the dress. Free from the clutches of the trailer hitch, I rolled to the side of the road like a roadkill squirrel.

Now, my biggest fear became the possibility that Linda would see me in a dress, so I began to hobble toward home as fast as a kid, whose knees had just about been scraped off, could hobble. Then in a rush I was swooped from the ground, and my mother carried me toward our house. I had never seen her so agile. Holding me cradled in her arms she leapt the stone wall, dodged the grape vines, and within a minute I was lying on the bed in the girls' room, and my sisters were protesting that I was bleeding on the blanket. They weren't feeling mean. It was their only blanket. I tried my best not to bleed.

In the blur, there were instructions, and my sisters ran off to a neighbor's to borrow the phone to call Doctor Marion. As the shock wore off, my knees began to hurt, and the pain continued to increase. I was grateful to hear the doctor's car in the driveway.

He pulled up a kitchen chair to the bedside and inspected

my knees.

"Hurts a bit, doesn't it?"

I nodded.

"We'll fix you up." He said to me, then stood and turned to my mother.

"Genny, we have to get those knees cleaned up, and there are tar and rocks and dirt embedded in there. It's going to take a while," He looked back at me for a few seconds then turned back to my mother and whispered, "And it's going to hurt like hell, but if we don't get it all an infection could cause him to…." I didn't hear the rest, but it didn't sound good.

He took a few small amber bottles and some gauze pads from his black doctor bag. My mother pulled a second chair next to the couch, put it in front of the doctor but closer to my head. She reached down and held both my shoulders, kissed me on the forehead and said, "You have to be tough, Johnny." She was crying. Then the pain by which I forever judged every other pain in my life began, as the doctor rubbed raw alcohol into the open wounds that used to be my knees. He started picking out the bigger pieces of gravel with tweezers and then doused the open wounds again with raw alcohol and rubbed. This went on for at least an eternity.

I screamed some, but mostly not. Instead, I prayed. When he was done, he stood up. He and my mother both had tears. He looked down and said, "You are one tough little Irishman."

I was never so proud of my heritage. Then came the words

that will live in infamy forever.

"See you tomorrow," he said, and he left the room.

The treatment went on for weeks. First, he came every day, then every few days, then he came and said he was finished. He said I should "take it easy" on my legs for a few days. He turned to my mother, and, as if I couldn't hear him because he had his back to me, he said, "If there is any infection, call me right away. If the infection is too deep, he might lose the use of that right leg. I think I got all the pieces and, well, time will tell."

Time told, and with confidence I prayed I wouldn't "lose the use of that right leg." I figured it would be hard to pitch with one leg. The knees scabbed over, and I went to play in the yard. Friends came to visit as if I were an invalid, and the mornings became brisk, but every time a car turned into the driveway my eyes watered, and I steeled my clenched teeth until I determined it wasn't the doctor coming back to rub my knees with alcohol.

But my family had other things to think about. No sooner had I returned to running, than my family was hit with chicken pox. I didn't get them, but my sisters did, and the Board of Health quarantined our family. For weeks people dropped off groceries at the top of the driveway up near the road. Then I would have to go up and get them and haul them to the house. I didn't mind. It gave me a chance to work my legs back into shape.

It was mid-December by the time we were free to go back

to school. When we were allowed back into society, there was a party at Grammy's, and Uncle Frankie and his family showed up. My uncles cleared the big room of furniture, except for chairs which they lined around the walls on the hardwood floor. Uncle Jim cranked up the Victrola, and we heard old Irish songs on crackly one-sided records and the Scottish singer Harry Lauder, supposedly for my mother, but Mum said it was probably for Grammy too. It was at this party that I got my first taste of Guinness, delivered by Cousin Sean while his father was dancing.

Then my old man stopped the record and said he'd give a toast. He raised his glass in the direction of Uncle Frankie, and in his best Irish brogue he said, "Avoid coming in contact with either the military or the police, they are only doing what they cannot help."

Everyone laughed, even Uncle Frankie.

I found out later it was itself a commandment. It was a rule of the Molly Maguires.

"To the Molly Maguires!" they all said in unison, but not the women. Then other toasts echoed "to Gallagher's Bar, "To a free Ireland," "To Father Cuddihy," and "To Skibbereen" where the Hourihans came from. The laughing and toasting continued until my grandfather, Cornelius Joseph O'Hourihane himself, stood and raised his glass. This didn't happen often. As a matter of fact, I seldom if ever had heard my grandfather speak.

"To me brothers," he said loudly, his bushy eyebrows

clenched and his Irish eyes flashing the anger of New York City in the 1800s, and everyone raised a glass. "Ta the Dead Rabbits," he nearly shouted.

No one laughed at this. They drank in silence. Then the music returned, and they all danced, and drank, and sang until everyone was ready for a Guinness nap, including some of the children.

## The Difference Between Martyrs

The following Monday in school, we began to learn about the Catholic Commandments. I had to admit that the first two were about things I had seen recently.

"One."

It was the first time it had occurred to me that I was going to have to kneel on my rehabilitating knees.

"Two."

I turned to the back of the room.

"Three."

"Sister, I can't," I blurted, and I turned toward her.

"What do you mean you can't? Get up on your chair."

I loved the nuns, but if you can't do something, you can't do it, no matter who commands it.

"I hurt my knees. And I don't think I can kneel on them."

"Do you think our martyrs complained about hurt knees?"

I figured they hadn't, but I still didn't think I could kneel on them.

"Three," she said again and looked directly at me.

I turned slowly, and asking God for help, I knelt up onto the wooden chair. It hurt, and they bled, but I did it, and I did it without tears.

"Which are the two great commandments that contain the whole law of God, children?"

"Sister, the two great commandments that contain the whole law of God are: Thou shalt love the Lord thy God with thy whole heart, and with thy whole soul, and with thy whole mind, and with thy whole strength; Thou shalt love thy neighbor as thyself."

"Children," she said softly, "If you forget everything else you are taught about your religion, remember these, and you will be doing well."

# CHAPTER 14
## The Story of Christmas

**CHRISTMAS WAS TO BE ON** Thursday, and although it was only Tuesday, I was already excited. Most people have no idea how wonderful Christmas is for an innocent Catholic child. Of course, there is school vacation, Santa Claus, presents, Gene Autry singing Rudolf, multi-colored lights, the tree, the cartoon show at the Salvation Army, fruitcake, and a large meal with family. Sometimes there are also snow, sleds and snow angels. But these things most every kid gets.

For a Catholic child there is that, but also midnight Mass, and the hymns echoing off the walls of a full church, Adeste Fideles on the organ, and the story of the birth of Jesus from the pulpit. There is the priest blessing at school, and the lights at the Fatima shrine a few towns over. No other holiday compares; Easter being a not-so-close second since there are no presents, but there's more candy.

At school, the priest visited our class and handed out boxes of hard candy and his blessing. We only got the blessing of the priest if one of our classmates asked him for it before he decided to leave the room. Sister always knew when Father Carbary was going to visit so she would designate someone to ask him for his blessing. It was always one of the rich kids. I figured it was more difficult for the priest to say no to someone whose family had donated a ton of money or some land or a building to the church, so it made sense. Today it was Donald Mulchahy. Father Carbary was a Skibbereen man himself, and I figured it would make more sense if one of his own kinsmen, such as myself, asked for his blessing, but I never petitioned Sister about it.

I was over-excited all day with having eaten an entire box of hard candy using the few teeth that had grown back in, and when it came time for bed, my sister Diane was designated to help me get to sleep, so she began to read me a story. I pulled the woman's green cloth winter coat I used as a blanket up to my neck as I nuzzled into my bed, and she sat at the edge with the book and read.

"The decree went out all across Israel that a census was to be taken. Joseph took his wife Mary, who was with child, on a trip to Bethlehem where they would be counted."

I pictured the young woman, on the nest like my mother had been so recently, riding on the back of a burro while Joseph led the animal by the reins across the expanse of night, across the front of the cardboard box that had contained the priest's hard candy, the cold stars in the blackness as a backdrop, and their road crossing the darkened hills.

"But there was no room at the inn, and Mary was made comfortable in the hay in the stable…"

My sister stopped reading, leaned over and gently put her arm around me, then called for my mother. When she arrived, my sister told her, "I was just reading the story of Christmas, and he started crying."

What my own pain from being dragged on my knees up our driveway and down an asphalt street couldn't produce, the pain in the story of the first Christmas had. I cried myself to sleep, and we never spoke of it again. Boys don't cry, especially Hourihan boys.

The next morning began Christmas Eve. We spent the day wrapping presents. We each had gifts for each sister and brother, for my mother and father, and for Grammy and Aunt Kathleen, who lived with Grammy and had no one. I guess it was because she always said, "Lips that touch wine will never touch mine," and she most likely didn't know any men who didn't drink. So she never got kissed, and therefore, never had a baby.

I would give my brothers and sisters an array of different colored stylus fountain pens with a few extra pen-points, or Number Two pencils each wrapped meticulously in Frosty the Snowman paper. I would give my father a package of brand new razor blades, and my mother was scheduled to get toilet water, but I had procured something myself for her. It was a can of crab meat. She loved crab meat. But, being round, it was real hard to wrap. I sat and watched the multicolored lights on the tree reflecting off the fake icicles and listened to a Gene Autry Christmas Special on the radio until it was okay to go to bed.

"Don't forget," my mother said, "As soon as every child is fast asleep Santa comes, and then it's morning."

When morning arrived, I stepped barefoot out of the Little Room into the half-light of the living room. I was stunned motionless, as if I had hit an invisible wall. The living room floor was completely covered by a blanket of wrapped presents. Somehow my mother always managed to fill up the entire floor with gifts, even when my father arrived home with half his paycheck gone to Tibby's. This year she had bought boxes of Crayolas and wrapped each crayon individually. We all got knitted socks, hats, slippers, mittens, scarves, and coloring books. My sisters got clothes and paper dolls, combs and brushes, barrettes for their hair, and a board game of Chinese Checkers. Dennis got the Great Garloo battery-operated robot and a cap gun and holster set, and standing in the corner was a present for me.

Even before opening it, I realized it was a Joe Palooka punching bag. This lesson-teacher of the pugilistic arts began with a flat metal piece a foot wide and three feet long lying tight to the floor. On one end was a metal rod that stood straight up about three and a half feet from the floor to the leather air-filled punching bag on top of the rod. I stood on the floor piece, wound up, and punched the bag with everything I had. It bent backwards, then snapped back and hit me square in the face. My nose started to bleed. I looked in shock at the parents who had bought me this mechanism of child torture. My father, who had spent part of his youth as a boxer, picked up a doll from my sister's pile of opened presents and tossed it to me. "Here, play with this," he said in disgust.

"Jack!" my mother admonished. She took the doll and gave it back to my sister while my father went to the kitchen to get some ice for my nosebleed. We put the ice in a sock, and I held it on the bridge of my nose as I watched Christmas happen from the couch while my sister Nancy complained that I was bleeding all over her sock. It seemed to me I was always bleeding on people's stuff.

After a while my nose stopped bleeding, and we packed up and went to Grammy's for dinner, and I opened her present to me.

"Yours is the one on the right side," Grammy said. "It has your name on it. Don't take the wrong one now. Read. Get the right one."

It was a brand new three-finger baseball glove, about which I could only say, "but it's left handed."

My mother shushed me, spirited away the glove, gave it to Aunt Adele who switched it with her left-handed son

Daryl's and everything was "hunky dory." To which I could only say, "But Daryl doesn't play baseball." Daryl cried, and my Uncle Jim called him "thick" and gave him a smack in the back of the head, so he stopped.

I looked around at my cousins. I counted them. There were twenty-four of us there that day ranging from babies to teenagers. We had all been hungry and thirsty in our young lives, and we had all worn shoes so small they hurt and clothes bought at auction. We had been cold and dirty, and, like original sin, we had been beaten and punished for things we didn't do by people we loved. But today it was Christmas, we were at Grammy's, and we were going to have potatoes, carrots, cabbage, and a slice of ham followed by bread pudding with raisins and whipped cream, and we were surrounded by cousins who knew us and accepted us for who we were. That made it all okay, at least for today. Before the Christmas party was over, a telephone call came. Neighbors had apparently been annoyed by the noise and had complained to the police. Uncle Dan answered the phone, listened for a moment, then held it out toward Grammy.

"Ma, it's Chief Mac. He says he'll only talk with you."

As my grandmother started across the floor to answer the phone, my uncle smiled and handed it toward my father as a joke, remembering his fabled donnybrook with the chief. They both laughed, but not a lot.

She took the phone and listened for a few minutes silently, then said, "That's good o' ya, Chief. Okay."

She handed the phone back to Uncle Dan and turned to the rest of us.

"Alright," she said. "Keep the noise down." She looked directly over my head at Uncle Frankie, who was standing behind me. "The neighbors are complainin'."

The phonograph was cranked up again, and the Carmel Quinn record was put back on, right in the middle of Mick McGilligan's Ball. We all went back to our party, and it didn't seem all that less noisy to me. A few minutes later Uncle Frankie and my two Holyoke cousins, Timmy and Mary, and Aunt Eve were all dressed in their winter coats and standing at the door saying goodbye to everyone. Uncle Frankie's family leaving the party was like a warmth being extinguished in the room. They were that much fun. But I guess they had to hurry off because they lived such a long drive away, even longer in winter.

My Uncle Frankie came across the room and hugged me that day. He never said why, just hugged me, tussled my hair and then left. I liked all my uncles, but he was my favorite. I guess he knew it.

# CHAPTER 15
## The Commandments Begin

***"I AM THE LORD THY God; thou shalt not have strange gods before Me.'*** That is the first of the ten Commandments of God, children. They are not suggestions. They are not debatable. They are commandments."

Sister Thomas Joseph, in her black and white habit, stood next to a rectangular two-foot by three-foot white poster board with ten Commandments meticulously printed in indelible black ink. She pointed to the first one with her black-tipped pointer. I sat in my back-row seat, blankly staring up to the front of the room at the list of commandments hanging next to the slate blackboard. I marveled at how everything in my vision was so black and white.

***Thou shalt not take the name of the Lord in vain.***
***Thou shalt keep holy the Lord's Day.***

"Now, repeat after me, I am the…" She stopped at the sight of my hand shooting up into the air with a question obviously attached.

She sighed. "Yes, Mr. Hourihan, you have a question. And I have to tell you that if it isn't a good question…"

"I know Sister, woe betide me. I'll be going to the Britannica."

A few kids laughed, but I was dead serious. I knew that when my own "inclination for evil" showed up, I was probably going to end up in the box and be sent to China.

"What is your question?"

"When I got hurt, Dr. Marion said I could pray to God all I wanted but without my medicine my knees weren't going to get better."

"Yes, John, but God made the medicine." She smiled. She seemed so proud of her answer, almost smug in having out-thought a six-year-old. I stared at her in disbelief. This wonderful nun, the font of all the knowledge in my world, from religion to geography to arithmetic, to coloring inside the lines, had totally missed my question. Her answer had nothing to do with what I was trying to ask.

"But Sister, Dr. Marion is a Catholic. He's at Mass every Sunday."

"Yes. We all know Dr. Marion. He is a good Catholic man?"

I let it drop, satisfied that there were some grown-up Catholics who believed in the power of medicine over the power of God; Catholics who missed the first commandment entirely. I was confused, but it seemed recently that I often was.

I nodded my feigned understanding, and she went on with the "repeat-after-me's."

When she was done with religion class, she picked up the statue of our blessed mother off her desk. It was made of white plastic that glowed purplish in the dark because of the radium that was cooked into the plastic. The base opened up, and inside was a white plastic rosary that also lit up in the dark. We had all put our names in a box on her desk, and each week she pulled one out. When your name came up, you got to take the statue home for a weekend, and you got to entice your whole family into saying the rosary together both nights while absorbing radium from the beads. Today, she didn't even look at the hat.

"This week the Blessed Mother goes to John Hourihan," she said. "Remember what Bishop Fulton J. Sheen says, 'The family who prays together stays together.'" She called me to the desk with one finger curling in much the same way as the Wicked Witch of the East did in the Wizard of Oz, which I had recently seen sitting in front of my Aunt Dot's TV with my cousins. The flying monkeys scared the hell out of me, causing me to sit catatonic in horror. I had to be taken into the next room and fed jelly-filled cookies until I "came to my senses."

Needless to say, I made for the desk as quickly as I could. She handed me the statue and smiled. As I returned to my desk carrying the blessed virgin, I couldn't help thinking about what Bazooka Joe said, "The family that chews together sticks together." I looked at Jake, and he seemed to be thinking the same thing, and we laughed.

"Is there something funny, boys?"

"Just happy, Sister," I said.

That night, after meatloaf, canned beets, and pinkish Kraft Dinner that my father had ill-advisedly called "modern art," my mother told me to go get the statue. She called my sisters into the living room. Dennis and the baby got out of it, but as soon as we were all together, she smiled and shouted, "Jack, could you come in here a minute?"

My father came into the room carrying the Record/American newspaper and still reading the racing form. He took one look, recognized the statue, turned on his heel, and began to leave.

"Jack, what kind of example would that be?"

He came back in. The two exchanged glances. His said, "I'll get you for this." Hers said, "That'll teach you to make fun of my dinner."

We all knelt and Sweet Genevieve, which is what most of her family called her, handed the rosary to Scrapper Jack, which is what everyone called him. He began, but when he got into the Hail Mary as far as "Thy womb Jesus," we all laughed. He finished and began the next prayer, and when he got to "Jesus" there was another eruption. A third time. This time even my mother laughed.

"Jesus Christ!" he bellowed. "What the hell are you all laughing at? Son of a bitch."

Dennis was laughing in the corner. Even as young as he was, he seemed to watch the family as if it were his own situation comedy. We never finished the rosary because every time my father got to "Jesus," it sounded as if he was swearing, and we all laughed. Before the end of the second decade some of us were in tears from laughing, and my mother hugged him and said, "It's all right, Jack. You tried."

He handed the statue to me, but I was still laughing. I dropped it, and the bottom broke and fell off. We taped it back on with shiny black electric tape. When I brought it back on Monday, Sister began the class with, "Thou shalt not take the name of the Lord thy God in vain," I couldn't help myself. It started as a giggle in my stomach. It climbed to my mouth which twisted into a crooked smile until it covered my face, and, as the class repeated the words, I laughed out loud in remembrance of Scrapper Jack Hourihan praying the rosary.

"Go stand in the corner, Mr. Hourihan." I did, but I kept laughing.

## Another Hand Basket to Hell

On a late January Sunday, we Hourihan children, all except Neil and Dennis, lined up in the kitchen for inspection prior to beginning our two-mile walk in the frigid sun to St.

Mary's Church for the 10:30 Mass. It was cold, and it was a long walk, but to miss Mass on Sunday or on holy days of obligation was a mortal sin. To walk there for the eight o'clock Mass would have meant we would have had to begin getting ready at about 5 a.m. Four girls had to get ready, and there was only one bathroom. I didn't need the bathroom that much. I would just get up, go pee behind the barn, throw on my clothes, and I was ready. To miss the eight o'clock Mass was only a venial sin, so we opted for that.

"Remember to keep holy the Lord's Day," rang in my memory, first in Sister's voice, and then in the jumble of first-grade voices in holy repetition. I loved Sundays. I wore my red and black cloth winter coat, a black fake leather cap with a bill shorter than a baseball cap, and fold-down brown fur earmuffs. My sisters were a unity of different colored cloth coats and knitted hats. We all had knitted mittens and red, green, or blue boots. I had black rubbers because I was "too big for my boots." And as my Aunt Kathleen often said, I was also sometimes "too big for my britches."

My mother wouldn't be coming this week. I was sure God would understand, since He was responsible for her having to watch the baby and Dennis. My father had stopped going at all, and Aunt Kathleen had pronounced that he was going "to hell in a hand basket." It seemed that between the declarations of Aunt Kathleen and Grammy, everyone was to get a turn in the hand basket to hell. Mom checked each of us then handed us each a dime to put in the "poor box," which meant to me that we couldn't be poor since I never saw any of that money coming back to us.

Winter Street was a holy place for us. It was where the school, the rectory, the statue of St. Joseph, the convent, and the church were, and of course there was the small parking lot down the street that Mr. Mulchahy, Donald Mulchahy's father, leased to the school "for a dollar a year" so the school would have a place for its annual fund-raising carnival. As we turned onto the most sanctified of all roads in Milford, I felt special. The church loomed impressively as we turned the corner and faced the Milford-pink-granite house of God. The huge polished oaken doors were swung open in the middle of the face of the church that grew straight up to the bell tower. The sun played off the stained-glass windows of religious scenes in blue, green, red, and yellow, and the walkway was, to me, the most inviting stretch of land in existence. We filed in and followed Patty to an empty pew halfway from the back door to the altar. I took off my hat, and my sisters placed handkerchiefs on their heads, secured them with bobby pins, and we began filing into the pew. I loved the smell of incense and the hush and mumble of hundreds of parishioners dutifully filling in the seats. As I was following in line, chronologically behind Nancy, I saw that Diane hadn't genuflected all the way to the floor. I cut quickly in front of the twins, tapped Diane on the back, and pointed out this venial sin to her.

"You didn't go all the way to the floor," I said. I was just trying in vain to keep her milk bottle totally white. As time progressed into her teen years, that would become a totally futile task, but at this time I figured I still had a shot. Diane turned her back on me, reached back and grabbed a fist full of my coat and dragged me into the pew. When we reached the point at which we would be sitting, she turned to me and said, "Now, kneel down and pray that I don't kill you before we get home."

Her smile said that she was kidding, maybe. Or maybe it was just so others wouldn't know what she was saying.

When the poor box, a small woven basket with a green felt lining stuck on the end of a pole, was thrust down the aisle to us at half-time by one of those men whose demons defied holy water, I marveled that there were dollar bills and fives and tens in the hopper. I thought of what just one of those tens would do for my family. It would take only one to pay for half our week's groceries. And this enlightening box told me there were people in this church who had so many of them they could just give some away like we did with dimes. Mass became a game of looking around the crowd and trying to figure out who had given the tens and who had given the dimes.

After Mass, while we younger ones were told to wait next to the cold granite church building while Patty went to buy the paper from the Renards, and Diane talked with the boys from her class who now flocked to her, I wondered if what the Renards were doing was considered working on the

Lord's Day. I decided it couldn't be, any more than us selling Christmas seals a few Sundays ago was considered working, since it was okay with the church.

I was overjoyed when I was told as we walked down Winter Street that we were going to meet Mom and Dad at Grammy's house, and that we would be allowed to stop at Chez Vous for donuts on the way. I liked this new existence where Dad worked, and we got to have donuts after church. As I began to suck the jelly out of a donut sitting at a table in the sun inside the window of the bakery shop, it occurred to me that I had seen the nuns in here and even Father Carbary himself, and since it was pretty evident that someone was working here, I guessed that either the people making the donuts and waiting on customers were not Catholic, or someone wasn't paying attention to that commandment we had just learned; about the Lord's Day and keeping it holy.

"I'm never going to work on Sunday," I said to my sister Sheila, since she was sitting next to me. She looked at me for several seconds as if I had just dropped in from outer space, then she said, "That's nice." Sheila, even as a single digit child, was destined to be a mother. She looked after my brothers and me nearly every day. She gave us our tablespoons of cod liver oil and castor oil. She put Mercurochrome on cuts, washed faces, shooed bees away, made sure we had food, and every once in a while, she just got fed up. Today must have been one of those times. Without speaking further, she gently pushed my hat from the table onto the floor and went back to her donut.

# CHAPTER 16
Honor Thy Mother and Thy Father

**ON FRIDAY, SISTER RESTED COMFORTABLY** in her chair, behind the large oaken desk, opened *The Baltimore Catechism* and read, *"Thou shalt honor thy mother and thy father... Thou shalt not kill... Thou shalt not commit adultery."*

She closed the book and looked at us. She folded her hands, fingers interlocked, on the desk in front of her.

"Those are the fourth, fifth, and sixth commandments of God, children."

She rose to her feet slowly, steadying herself by placing her right hand on the edge of the desk for stability the way we all did when we knelt on the chairs. Somehow, from the look on her face, I knew it was more painful for her to stand than for us to kneel.

"I was an orphan," she said. "So, whom was I to honor?"

A wisp of gray hair had found its way out from under the habit-hat that she wore, and her bib was on crooked, as if she had had a difficult time dressing this morning.

We all looked at each other. We hated these questions that didn't have an answer in the book. Sister limped across the front of the room, observing each face as if she was looking for a question in someone's face rather than an answer on someone's lips.

"Mr. Calmini, whom was I commanded to honor, if I had no mother and no father?"

Carl had an Italian name and was here at St. Mary's by the grace of his mother, who was Irish and not by his Italian father, who had moved to Canada.

"I don't know."

"I need an answer. Am I to honor no one?"

Carl was fidgeting now. "I don't know. God?"

"Well, yes, but whom else?"

I thought of my cousins Daryl and Barbara. My Aunt Adele and Uncle Jim had adopted them, and then it came to me. I raised my hand. Sister smiled as if she knew what I was thinking.

"Yes, Mr. Hourihan?"

"You honor the people who brought you up."

"I was brought up in an orphanage."

"Then honor the people who took care of you?"

"That is correct. God puts some people in charge of us who

worry about our welfare and our health. This commandment tells us to respect and love and obey them." There was a pause, and she backed up to the desk to steady herself again. "Honor them, that is, in all that is not sinful. That is what this commandment means." She hobbled back to her chair and sat down. "And Carl, if you only have one parent, you honor her twice as much."

I guess Sister didn't know the horrible way Carl treated his mother.

She had very little to say about "Thou shalt not kill" except to say it included suicide, and she had nothing at all to say about adultery, so I asked my cousin Sean at recess.

"It's when you screw somebody," he said with a smirk as we ate our bag lunches sitting against the stone wall that encircled the playground. For warmth, we sat next to the fully inflamed stone incinerator.

"What?"

"Adultery is when you put your dick into a girl's beaver, and you do it."

This was very strange news to me, since I only had a slight idea what a beaver was.

"That is wrong. You're full of crap."

"It's true. It's how people get babies."

Now, I knew he was full of crap. That was just plain gross. If this was real, there wouldn't have to be a commandment against it because no one in their right mind would do it. It would be like having a commandment that said, "Thou shalt not piss uphill in your bare feet."

"You're such an asshole," I said. I stood, crumpled my bag, and tossed it into the burning incinerator. I decided if God wanted me to know what adultery was, He would tell me.

## Honoring Thy Father

This was not just another ordinary Sunday afternoon at Grammy's house. Sean and I had locked my younger cousin Curt, Aunt Pamela's son, in the under-stairs compartment outside where the garbage cans were kept. Curt was now peering out through the white crosshatch of strips of wood that were two of the sides. This wasn't in any way Curt's fault. We liked him well enough, but there was exactly enough room for the two steel garbage cans, a few lawn tools, three grocery bags of junk, and room left over just big enough for Curt. It seemed only right that we should lock him in. Then we went and sat on the front stairs. People didn't usually use the front stairs on Sunday, but there they were; my father and my uncles leaving the house.

"Hi Dad," I said, surprising him enough so he tripped on the last step and stumbled onto the front lawn, nearly falling down.

"Hey, Jocko." He straightened up. "Me and your uncles are going… to the store."

"Can I come?"

"Not this time," he said, and the five others laughed, like me and Jake did when we were enjoying an unspoken joke.

"Oh, let him come," my Uncle Dan said and laughed.

The group hustled off down Otis Street toward town, laughing. My father shoved his older brother Dan from behind. Only Uncle Mick stopped. Uncle Mick was my father's best friend and was married to my Aunt Alana, the oldest of my father's sisters.

Uncle Mick put his hand gently on my shoulder.

"Johnny, why don't you and Sean go back upstairs?" He looked over my shoulder and added, "And let Curt out of there before you go up." He laughed a little, waved to Curt who was valiantly fighting off the urge to cry, and hustled to catch up with the brothers Grimm.

Sean and I waved to Curt too, and then we sat back down on the front stairs.

"Where's your hat?" Sean asked, looking at the top of my bare head.

Although I lost my hat more often than I didn't, I hadn't realized that I wasn't wearing it.

"Don't know."

"Where do you remember it last?"

"At the donut place. I must have left it on the table."

"Let's go get it."

Chez Vous was all the way back uptown, almost all the way back to the church. We both knew this was a bad idea, but Sean cemented it in our heads when he said, "C'mon. I know a shortcut." We left Curt under the porch and walked off down the street.

The "shortcut" was actually a bit longer than walking straight down Main Street. We would walk up Otis to Chapin, then across to Forest, take a left on Claflin, hit North Bow Street which would bring us to the church, and a final left on Main would bring us to Chez Vous. This way we could stop at "the store," which we suspected was Tibby's Bar on North Bow, and see if our fathers were there. They weren't, so we retrieved my hat and walked home, almost without incident.

Claflin Street was a hill that cars couldn't get up in the winter even with chains, so the town closed it off and let kids sled down it. At the end was a stone wall, and if you didn't stop your sled in time that would be your last downhill trip for the winter.

Today, the street was empty. As we trekked up it, I continually eyed the gray asphalt-shingled home at the top. I knew once we arrived at the towering Victorian that we would begin downhill all the way to Grammy's house.

We arrived at the top, and I sat down on the grass and leaned back against the wrought-iron fence surrounding the towering, three-story house that sat in what appeared to be perpetual shadows. Sean sat beside me, and we rested.

"Hey boys," said a gravelly voice from inside the house.

I heard it from behind me, but when I turned all I saw was the dark gray home with the black shutters. Lace curtains, yellowing with age and cigarette smoke, hung in each window, and in one window at the right edge of the porch the curtain was pulled aside.

A face appeared in the darkness of the open window. It was an old face. Longish white hair was combed along the sides of his head, beginning at the part in the middle and tucked over each huge ear. His nose grew geriatrically down his face much longer than it should have been, and dark spots decorated any visible patch of skin.

"Hey boys, come here."

Sean and I looked at each other and then back at the old man in the window.

"Come here, damn it!"

Sean looked at him, assessed him, and then his head began to shake "No" even before he spoke. "I don't think so," he said and got up from the stone wall to leave.

I couldn't make myself retreat just yet. He was an old man, and he was inside the window. What harm could be done by a walk over to see what he wanted?

"Come on," I said to Sean. "Let's see what he wants."

We walked cautiously up the wooden steps and crossed the creaking porch, standing far enough away so that he couldn't reach out and grab us.

"You gotta get me outta here," he said, blinking one eye as he spoke. His eyes were bright blue and watery, and a wisp of his hair fell down across the one eye that kept blinking.

"Go to the front door. It's unlocked. Go inside, take a right and come push me the hell outta here. I gotta get home. I don't belong here. You have to help me escape."

It was only then that I noticed he was in a wheelchair.

"If you don't belong here, why doesn't your family come get you?" Sean asked.

"Because my family put me here, you moron."

He laughed a little too much, not a real laugh but as if he was stuttering the word "help." "He he he he he." Sean pulled at my coat, but I pulled back.

"What is this place?" I asked the man in the window.

"It's where families put old people they don't want any more. Do you know where Water Street is? I live on Water Street."

Sean added from behind me, "It's an old-age home… come on, let's go."

I let Sean pull me slowly across the porch to the stairs.

"You little bastards, get me outta here!" the old man shouted as we scuffled down the stairs and back to the sidewalk.

"You're both gonna burn in hell!"

I figured he was probably right. These Catholic rules were panning out to be pretty hard to follow. We ran the rest of the way back to our grandmother's house, where within minutes my mother hustled my family into a taxi, Mom and Patty in the front with the baby, the rest of us in the back, and about fifteen minutes later, after a severe scolding for having locked my cousin under the stairs, the taxi was crunching down our own driveway.

Dad didn't come home until later.

## Our Father Who Art at Gallagher's Bar

I woke in the middle of the night to my frigid black room and to my father's cold voice.

"Open this fecking door!" he shouted.

I turned over in bed and pulled the coat up over my head.

"Why don't you go back to the bar?" my mother shouted back.

"It's closed. Open the door or I'll kick it in." My father's voice changed when he was drunk, as if he had killed his conscience or at least knocked it out. It came from deep in his throat, and the music was gone.

"Go away," I heard my mother shoot back at him as she returned to her bedroom. "Sleep in the barn!"

There was the thud of a boot at the door, then the crash of shattering the glass. He was plastered again. Three sheets to the wind. Being true to his word, my father had tried to kick in the door. When it didn't work, he punched in the window, reached in, and unhooked the lock. By the time I got out to the kitchen, he had hold of my mother's bathrobe at the throat and was pulling her toward the stove. In his other hand, he held a knife.

I had been told many times how Hourihans were "the descendants of warriors," so I summoned my warrior blood and pushed myself between them. I started punching him in the stomach with all I had. His stomach was as high as I could reach. He let go of my mother and backed away. He looked down at me and tossed the knife onto the counter.

"Okay, okay, okay. It's okay. Pull up your drawers and go to bed."

I didn't. I pulled up my pajamas, which from the commotion had dropped some on my hips, and I stepped backwards but didn't leave the room. I leaned against the wall and waited. My sisters stood in a group in the door to the living room, just out of reach of the light from the kitchen. Dennis, being the smartest of all of us, stayed in bed.

Dad turned back to my mother. "Make me some eggs!"

"Make them yourself!"

It occurred to me that night that perhaps it was my mother who was a descendant of warriors; maybe of William Wallace himself. But then, we all knew what had happened to him. He got disemboweled. I didn't know what that meant, but it sure didn't sound like fun.

"I will beat you within an inch of your life," he growled.

He turned back to me. "I told you to go to bed, boyo, before I slap you silly!"

My father sometimes said the most frightening things, but I stood still against the wall.

As wonderful a man as my father was when he was sober, he was one mean drunk, and he had been at Gallagher's Bar uptown all Sunday afternoon and into the night. Tonight, no one was going to get any sleep. He was driven by guilt, depression, frustration, drink, and the universal Irish desire to return to the past. Most often these nightly ordeals were just screaming, name calling, and how he was going to beat so-and-so senseless, and how he wasn't going to take any more of so-and-so's guff, but sometimes people got hurt. I slid down the wall and sat on the floor to watch in fear of being beaten and determination to protect my mother. He tried to cook himself eggs, burned himself, and threw the cast iron frying pan across the kitchen. It bounced off the wall and slid under the table. He stumbled and bumped into the kerosene bottle attached to the stove. It wobbled.

"Jack, if you knock that over it will burn the house down," my mother admonished from her seat at the kitchen table where she was smoking a cigarette.

"Might not be such a bad thing," he slurred and eyed the bottle of fuel as if he had intentions of just kicking it over and ending everything. "At least our last night would be warm. Why is it so feckin cold in here?"

"We ran out of oil again."

For the next few hours, he shouted, he kicked things, he tried again to make eggs and failed. This time he just left them burning on the stove. He went to the kitchen table and sat down, crossed his arms in front of himself, leaned down and went to sleep right there. My mother got up, walked to the stove, and shut off the burner. She slid the eggs onto a plate and put them in front of her sleeping husband. Then she hustled us all to bed, and the night became quiet. It was a good night. No one had gotten hurt.

When we were all in bed, my mother came into my room. She knelt down beside the bed and whispered, "You're a good boy… but he's a bit big for you yet. Let me take care of it next time, okay?"

She left.

"Our Father, who art in heaven, hallowed be thy name," I thought as I drifted into sleep again. I loved this religion; it had an answer for just about every question a six-year-old could ask.

# CHAPTER 17
Thou Shalt Not Kill

**WHEN THE BRIGHT WHITE FEBRUARY** sun blasted through my window the next morning, bringing light but not heat, I got up. I hurriedly put on my coat and shoes, and wearing only my underwear, walked out the back door and behind the barn to pee. The cesspool was full again. The toilet didn't work so well, and I had decided cold was better than the smell. I had heard people talk about how they were "freezing their asses," but this morning I chuckled because I knew how it actually felt. I walked back in the front door which was still unlocked. Inside, I got the broom and a piece of cardboard and pushed the glass pieces from the floor in the mud room onto the cardboard with the broom. It wasn't necessarily my job to clean up my father's mess, but I was worried that someone would step in the glass in bare feet and get cut. As I dumped the glass shards into the brown paper garbage bag in the corner, I noticed my father was asleep on the floor in the other corner of the kitchen leaning against a pillow and covered with his coat.

I walked to the living room and noticed something else I hadn't seen last night. Uncle Lou was sleeping on the couch. Uncle Lou was my mother's uncle, not really ours, but he was one of our favorites. He lived up in the woods of Maine, but he came down to visit the bars of Milford sometimes, and on those occasions, he came home with my father and slept on the couch.

As the rest of the house began to rise, Uncle Lou chased us kids around. It was a tradition. When he caught one of us, he would let his upper false teeth drop from the roof of his mouth and they would chomp against the bottoms. It would scare the bejeezus out of us every time. Lou was in his late thirties, but he looked old to us, and with his wispy and thinning brown hair all tangled from a night on the couch, his teeth dropped from the roof of his mouth, and his arms outstretched as if to catch and eat whoever was in front of him, well, we ran and screamed and ran until my mother called us to breakfast.

Over oatmeal he told stories of World War II, "the big one."

He was in the Navy Construction Battalion, the Seabees, and as my father said, "He saw a lot of action."

## Baltimore Catechism: Clean Slate (Fall and Rise of a Catholic Boy)

Seabee my dog was named after Uncle Lou, since he brought him to our house and gave him to us as long as we named the dog Seabee. As I poked at my cereal, he talked about a place called Okee Nawa, and then he said he was sent to a new place called "Tin Man" where, "We were some of the first GIs on the island, and our job was to build a big shed where we would put together a secret weapon. It was 1945. We helped unload this new weapon from the Indianapolis. That was a big boat, not the city. We put it in the barn we built, and then we weren't allowed to go inside anymore. Instead, we got to pull guard duty around it. A few guys got to go in, but they weren't much for talking about what was in there. I pulled guard duty every night. Then, one day they put that atomic bomb on a plane and took it to Hiroshima, dropped it, and blew the damn place to hell. Killed about 50,000 people with one swipe. Taught those Japs a lesson."

I knew from my uncles' stories, and from my father's guilt at not having gone, that there had been a war just before I was born, and I knew it was against the heathen Japanese who reportedly "put no value on a man's life," but I had never before understood that relatives of mine, Scottish, French, and Irish Catholics from Milford, Massachusetts, people who had attended St. Mary's, had actually killed people with an atomic bomb. I thought only the godless Russians would do something like that. I thought of Japanese school children putting their heads under coats to stop the blast and then dying.

"You killed them?" I blurted over my cooling oatmeal, across the table, past his coffee, and right into his stunned face. "You killed them? It was our atomic bomb? We did it?"

It was too late. The cat was out of the bag.

"'Fraid so, Johnny. We killed a lot of them. They deserved it. Did you know the Japs sunk that boat, the Indianapolis, and about 700 of the sailors got eaten by sharks?"

"Okay, Uncle Lou, that's enough," my mother said.

"But, Thou shalt not kill," I said. "It's a commandment! It's not a suggestion!"

I left my half-eaten cereal on the table and ran outside, because Hourihan boys didn't cry, and my eyes were beginning to water. The dog followed me.

Now, I didn't know those Japanese people from Adam, and although killing them still bothered me, what was bothering me most was that Uncle Lou and all those Seabees were going to hell in a hand basket, too. My family was dropping like flies.

## Joshua Fit the Battle of Jericho

I went to school planning to get some explanation about this commandment from the good sisters, but instead, things got worse. There was a new kid on the bus, so I sat with him to make him feel not so alone.

"Hi," he said hopefully as I sat down.

"Hi, I'm John Hourihan."

"Josh Zielinski."

"That's not Irish, is it?"

"No. Polish."

When we got off the bus, he followed me right into my class.

"Children," Sister said to quiet us in our seats. Josh was standing right next to her in the front of the class. She had her hand on the back of his neck.

"This is Joshua Zielinski. He comes to us from a town near Holyoke where the retired sisters live. He is going to be in our class now, and as a sort of welcoming, Sister Superior is here to tell us about his namesake, Joshua of the Bible."

I loved the Bible stories, turning water into wine, healing the sick, raising the dead, walking on water. Sister Superior was old, very old. I sometimes wondered if the Bible stories she told were just her remembering them from when she was a little girl. When I told my mother this, she said I should ask Sister, but I didn't. I smelled a trap. Sister Superior looked like a happier version of the witch in the *Snow White and the Seven Dwarfs* book, only her hat was flat on the top and she had the white bib thing, but she was bent over like the witch, and she was shorter than all the other nuns. I had wondered upon entering the class why she had been standing in the corner of the room, smiling. I almost expected her to offer us an apple. Now she dragged a chair to the front of the class and sat down, opened her book, smiled at us one more time, and read.

She told of how Moses had died, and Joshua took over as the leader of the Israelites (which I always assumed was another name for the Irish, since they were the good guys in the Bible.) She read how he crossed the Jordan and faced the walled city of Jericho, and how God told him that the Israelites should march around the city's walls, and on the seventh time they should all shout and the trumpets should be blown. Sister read with reverence, occasionally punctuating the story with a smile and a nod of appreciation for the holy Israelite army.

"So all the people making a shout, and the trumpets sounding, when the voice and the sound thundered in the ears of the multitude, the walls forthwith fell down (nod, smile): and every man went up by the place that was over against him: and they took the city, (nod, smile) and killed all that were in it, man and woman, young and old. The oxen also and the sheep, and the asses, they slew with the edge of the sword."

She looked up, smiling the smile of the self-righteous, of the victorious.

*They killed everyone?* I wasn't smiling.

"But sister, they weren't supposed to kill everyone, were they?"

"Yes, child." Sister Superior smiled in my general direction. I didn't think she could actually see me, but she had obviously heard a voice in the left side of room. "It was a war. People die in wars. It's different."

"But God ordered them to kill everyone, and God ordered 'Thou shalt not kill'... How did they know when to do what?"

Sister Thomas Joseph stepped from the corner where she had been standing in the shadows. "Sister Superior has to go now." She extended her arms, palms up at her waist, then raised them, and we all stood up in unison and recited, "Thank you, Sister Superior."

"You are welcome, children." She smiled and left noiselessly except for the rustle of her habit.

I went to the bus and home that afternoon confused that there was a commandment from God that was indeed a suggestion and obviously very debatable. Josh sat with me on the bus, and as soon as his butt hit the seat he turned and said, "Wow. You're right. They just killed all those people because they were from somewhere else. Do you think that still happens?"

I told him what Uncle Lou had said about the Japs, and we both fell silent somewhere around Dilla Street halfway to my home.

A few forkfuls into dinner I stopped eating, placed my fork on the table beside my Chinese food from a can, and said with conviction, "Mom, I'm never going to kill anyone—even if God tells me to. Do you think that would be okay?"

My sisters didn't even raise their heads. They just did what they always did when I said things like this. Their eyes would drift in my direction for a second or two and then to each other. They would smile at each other and sometimes shake their heads. Then they continued to eat their "chopped suey," but now with a smile. Dennis laughed out loud. He seemed to know too much for a little kid.

"I think that would be okay, Johnny. Actually, I think it might be preferable," said Sweet Genevieve.

I wasn't sure what that last word meant, but this made it easier than explanations of WWII or Jericho. Thou shalt not kill. For me it would be a commandment, and when it came to killing, I prayed to God that He would just leave me out of the loop.

# CHAPTER 18
Adultery Is for Adults

MY MOTHER, THE TWINS, AND I were playing Whist at the kitchen table when I thought I heard the sound of horse's hooves outside. There were only a few horses left in the neighborhood. One of them was from way up the top of Purchase Street by the cemetery, and the other was owned by Mrs. Herman from down the street.

My mother must have heard it too, since she stopped shuffling for a few seconds and listened, then finished shuffling. I watched her head as she looked to her left out the window to see my father leave the barn where he had been pulling nails out of boards and straightening them to be used later. Her eyes followed him across and in front of the house. She waited a few seconds and leaned forward so she could see down the pantry and out the windows at the far end of the house. When she saw him walk around the front and down the side, she put the cards down without dealing and said, "Girls, go out and find your father."

Nancy and Sheila got up in confusion. "What should we do with him when we find him?" Nancy asked.

"You won't have to do anything. Just go say hi."

"No more cards?" I asked.

"Do you want to play war?" From the expression on her face, I wasn't sure she meant the card game.

"No. I think I'll go find Dad, too."

"Good, go ahead."

I stepped outside the front door, took an abrupt turn, and circled the house back toward the way from which my father had come. At the back of the house, I met with a wonderful surprise. A beautiful horse stood in the field between our yard and Linda's grandfather's berry garden.

It was a dark brown shining quarter horse, rippled with muscles, a perfect mane, and a tail just a little darker than the rest of him. Sitting atop this icon of the Wild West was Mrs. Herman, and my father behind her, on the horse, his arms around her waist. Nancy and Sheila had indeed found Dad, and they were standing at the head of the horse looking up at him quizzically. Mrs. Herman had hair blacker and shinier than the horse's mane and bright blue eyes that I could see shining from fifteen yards off. She was small and thin except for her chest, and watching her sit on that horse made me think how much fun it was to see her.

"Wow," I shouted, "what a great horse!"

"Maybe this isn't a good time," my father said to Mrs. Herman.

"Rain check?" she asked. Whatever that meant.

"Rain check," he acknowledged and slipped to the ground.

My father had always wanted to be a cowboy. He loved Country and Western music, especially Hank Williams' *Honky Tonk Man*. His favorite book was *The Man from Skibbereen*, about a cowboy Irishman who had come to America from the same town in Ireland that had been my grandfather's home. It seemed, as he dismounted, that he had really wanted to take a ride on this beautiful animal, but instead, as he stood beside it, he reached up and patted Mrs. Herman on the leg then slapped the horse on the ass and watched her bound away. He put his arms around each of my sisters and walked back toward the house. I watched until I could no longer see the horse or the woman, then I went inside. My mother and father were sitting at the kitchen table. The girls were nowhere in sight. I heard him say, "Cheech beat her again last night. She just wanted someone to talk to."

Mom absently shuffled the cards again. "Then maybe she should…" My mother turned and looked at me as I began to pull up a chair. "Skedaddle!" she said and meant it. There was obviously something going on here that I didn't understand any more than I had understood, "Thou shalt not commit adultery."

When you grew up, weren't you supposed to become an

adult? I loved this religion, and I wanted more than anything to do what it told me, but it sure was becoming confusing.

## CHAPTER 19
Thou Shalt Not Steal

**IT WAS DURING THE LATE** February thaw. For me, it was the best part of the week, Saturday TV time. I was perfectly happy, dressed in corduroys and a T-shirt, fed a bowl of Cream of Wheat, and sitting on the floor, leaning back against the arm of the couch, watching the black and white Zenith. Suddenly, my teeth clenched and my heart began to race, and I didn't know why until I looked out the window from the living room to see Dr. Marion's car rolling down the driveway. I must have heard it before I saw it.

I felt a sudden twinge in my knees. I turned back to the TV and an episode of a new show, Wild Bill Hickock. I wished, almost out loud, that the TV show was life, and I could crawl inside the tube and turn off the doctor's arrival. Maybe if I refused to believe he was here, he would just go away. But he came directly into the living room with my mother. He wore a crumpled gray suit and a black tie, and his glasses clung to his nose and ears as if in fear of falling.

"The doctor wants to see your knees." He walked to the couch where I was sitting, knelt down on the floor, and rolled up my pant legs. He looked for a few minutes, unrolled my pant legs to cover them back up, rose, and turned to my mother.

"Great," he said, smiling. "They healed great. I don't know, maybe I can see the other kids while I'm here. Just a wellness visit. Happy to waste the trip."

We all lined up. He checked our throats, looked in our ears and eyes, and listened to our chest and back. Since everyone except Dennis and Neil was old enough to be in school, we were all very good at lines. Then the doctor turned to my mother and said, "You know Genny, I think they could use some vitamins, maybe a one-a-day. They could use some vitamin C, and I'm going to leave some cod liver oil and castor oil for tummy aches."

My mother thanked him as he emptied his bag of pretty much every sample he had. She handed him a dollar, which he refused to take, then he climbed into his car and left. I watched him from the threshold of the front door and thought how charitable that had been of him. He must have bought that stuff, and he just gave it to us. I supposed it was because we were some of those people who put dimes in the poor box, and he put fives and tens.

A few days later, we had what would come to be known as our Tropicana snowstorm. We had had orange juice before, but usually it came from oranges someone had given to us at Grammy's that you cut in half and squeezed on the orange squeezer, earning only a few sips before it was gone. But during our Tropicana snowstorm it was different, and I was sure something had gone on that we didn't know about.

It was as black a six o'clock in the afternoon as I had ever seen when my father trudged down the snow-covered driveway using the stone wall for direction, through a nor'easter, carrying a smile and a large box. My mother held the door open for him, and he stepped inside, shook the snow off his shoulders, and walked into the kitchen. He smiled at my mother as he put the box on the table and opened the top. Inside were twenty-four quarts of Tropicana orange juice.

"Jack!"

"It fell off a truck," he blurted. "I was right up the top of the driveway, and the truck went by, hit a pothole, and this box jumped right out of the back. Fell right in the driveway. I think it was a gift from God."

"Sure it was," she said.

"Hey, I'd bring it back, but I didn't get the number of the truck."

"I suppose it said Tropicana on the side?"

"You know, I think it did."

He laughed. She shook her head and turned to me. "Get

some glasses." They smiled at each other. I never found out where that orange juice came from, but I was pretty sure it hadn't jumped off a truck.

After a few days of orange juice with breakfast, it didn't matter much where it had come from. The doctor had said to "increase our vitamin C," and here it was; a gift from God. That night, I watched the snow fill up the driveway, then the garden. It started climbing up the steps. Before the night was over, nearly a foot-and-a-half had fallen. To make matters even more heavenly, the temperature rose for a short time, and the snow turned to rain. The temperature then plummeted, and the foot-and-a-half of snow was covered with an inch-and-a-half of ice.

In the morning, just after hearing on WORC radio that school would be called off, I was the first to find out that our metal-runner sleds could be pushed off from the stone wall on the other side of our driveway, and I could speed down the hill, across the entire expanse of the baseball diamond in Gonhue's field, over the walking bridge, and into Spike's yard, past the chicken coops and into the next yard. I didn't even know who owned that yard, so I guessed I was exploring.

The runners never broke through the ice layer, and the sled continued to pick up speed until the wind it created blew my eyes fluid and blurred the expanse of white ice ahead. The walk back was an eternity, with my feet refusing traction, and the sled sliding side to side, tugging at my arm with every step.

"Where have you been?" my sister Patty asked as I shivered

into the kitchen.

"Sliding."

"Must be real good."

"Real fast, and I went all the way to the house next to Spike's, but it is hard to steer, and the walk back was pretty slippery. It's a great ride, but you just have to make sure you don't fall off the sled halfway there."

I dropped my coat on the floor next to the radiator.

"It's not on," Patty said.

I touched the cast iron radiator and found it cold.

I walked to the kerosene cooking stove, turned on the burner with a wooden match, and warmed my hands. On the next burner was a pan of oatmeal. I stuck my finger in. It was still warm, so I got a bowl of it and sat at the kitchen table to eat. Through the window I saw the smoke pouring from Spike's chimney and wished to God I was visiting or at least had his fireplace. We had only had enough money to fill the oil tank half way, and the oil had run out again. It was going to be a cold night. I pulled my coat back on and offered it up for the souls in purgatory.

## CHAPTER 20
Thou Salt Not Cover Thy Neighbor's Wife

**RELIGION CLASS BECAME SHORTER DURING** this time as we prepared for the upcoming science fair. We had to study science sometime. Science being the way God does stuff.

My project was on the water cycle, where water runs down the mountains into the ponds and lakes and oceans, then it is sucked up into the air and forms clouds, and then the clouds rain cats and dogs down on us and everything gets soaking wet, like the day the kitchen window was left open, and we lost all the sugar, baking soda, and flour. Then the water starts its cycle all over again. God is great.

I had snuck out of the school yard at lunchtime and gone to Cahill's stationery store on Main Street and bought a poster cardboard, some tempera paints, a brush, and a number two pencil. The whole thing cost a whopping twenty-six cents. It had taken me three weeks to save enough, but I was sure God and the poor people would understand. While I waited for science class when we would get to work on our "projects," I half listened to Sister's explanation of the seventh, eighth, ninth, and tenth commandments.

*"Thou shalt not steal,"* she said.

Jake raised his hand.

"Sister," he asked when called on. "What if it is medicine or food that you need to keep alive?"

The sisters were the most empathetic people I had ever met, and her look of compassion now was punctuated by the way she began blinking away tears. Being a Hourihan boy and bound by Hourihan law not to cry, I could tell in a second when someone was blinking away tears. They stopped talking, swallowed hard, and then they blinked several times before they could speak again. I even knew how it felt.

"Jacques, we are never to steal, never to take something that doesn't belong to us. If we truly need the medicine or the food, God will provide. Just have faith."

*Like the Tropicana*, I thought, a gift from God.

My friend nodded his acceptance if not his understanding.

She went on. *"Thou shalt not bear false witness against thy neighbor.* Do we know what that means?"

Half the class answered in various forms of, "We shouldn't lie about people."

That was basic. We had all been told by our parents and older sisters that we shouldn't lie, but from this day forward, it was a commandment from God himself. I looked across at Jake, and he raised his right eyebrow as he did a lot. It made me laugh out loud, as it always did, and Sister bustled down the aisle.

"Is there something funny, Mr. Hourihan?"

"No, Sister," I lied, and only seconds after I had found out about the commandment from God. So she went back up the aisle without whacking my knuckles with the pointer. I guess she forgot.

As she walked back toward the front of the room she continued. "***Thou shalt not covet thy neighbor's wife, or thy neighbor's goods.***"

It occurred to me that her attack down the aisle might have just been a pre-emptive strike in anticipation of this new commandment. This just made no sense at all. Maybe she didn't want me to ask the logical question, the one that must have been on the mind of every kid in the class, "Sister?" I called to her back. She spun, glared, and then quickly gathered herself and said calmly, "Yes, Mr. Hourihan?"

"What if it's raining?"

"What?" she shouted as she became, just as quickly, ungathered.

There was no empathy in her voice now. She wanted to know what the hell I was talking about. Jake laughed, but he wasn't punished.

"What if it's raining? Wouldn't God want us to cover our neighbor's goods and his wife so they don't get soaked? Once, we lost all our flour, sugar, and baking soda that way."

She didn't even say a word this time, just pointed to the corner, and I realized this had nothing to do with wanting me to understand what she was saying. It had nothing to do with me being overly energetic. She was punishing me, plain and simple, and I had no idea why. I thought it was a darned good question.

"God damn," I said under my breath.

"What did you say?" she shouted and moved toward me, her black habit rustling against each chair in the aisle like Jesus must have done when He found money changers in the temple.

"I said, 'Yes ma'am,'" I lied. It seemed like the right thing to do, commandments notwithstanding.

"Oh," she said and went back to the front of the class.

At lunch, I told Jake I didn't like peanut butter, and he said he would eat half of my sandwich for me. He did the same with my apple. He was a good friend that way.

## Father Knows Best

That afternoon after school, I asked my mother why I had been punished.

"Covet," she said, accentuating the "t".

I was still confused.

"It means that you are not allowed to want the things, the goods, that your neighbors have."

"What about coveting thy neighbor's wife?"

"Yeah," she said then thought for a few minutes. "Right," she finally decided. "You should ask your father about that one."

I never did ask him, though. Again, I smelled a trap. Why would anyone covet his neighbor's wife? Isn't one enough? And besides, I didn't think you could even have two. I think it's against the law. Everything had been so clear to me at the beginning of this school year. I loved the safety and beauty of this Catholic religion, but some of the rules made no earthly sense whatsoever, and I was trying my best to figure out how a human being could go by them. It seemed everyone wanted us to act like Jesus, but it didn't seem fair. After all, He was God, and we were just kids.

Dr. Marion had his god of medicine, but the nuns considered him to be a good Catholic man. My father and his brothers took the Lord's name in vain between syllables of individual words, but they bowed their heads at the mention of Jesus' name, and the church set up Catholics to work on Sunday selling newspapers. People put their fathers in old age homes against their will, and it was difficult to honor a father who got drunk on payday and terrorized his family all night. It seemed it was okay with the church to kill Japanese people as long as we called it a war, and even God told people to kill each other, especially Canaanites. People stole and lied about it like the orange juice, and they lied about other people all the time, and everyone coveted everything other people had. For God's sake, even I coveted Spike's fireplace when we ran out of oil in the middle of the winter. I didn't see how anyone could possibly make it to heaven if we had to go by these rules. But, under my bed that night, listening to my father shout about how he was going to choke my sister "silly" if she didn't shut up and make him some "feckin" eggs and toast, I decided I would try to be the one who did it. Not the eggs and toast, but the one who made it to heaven. Although, it seemed that heaven must be a lonely place with everyone going to hell in a hand basket.

At breakfast my mother nearly choked herself silly when I announced I was going to be a priest. She coughed, swallowed hard, and then laughed even harder when I explained, "Of course, I mean when I grow up, not right away."

About a month later, when Sister was explaining "the calling," by which is meant when God "whispers in your ear" that you should become a priest or a nun, I walked brazenly up to her desk at the beginning of lunch time. It seemed she was trying to ignore me, but I stared at her until she turned to me.

"Yes?"

"Sister, do you think I have the calling?"

Her head twisted, she grabbed her crucifix, her chin dropped, her mouth opened, and her eyes widened as she quickly blessed herself. "Oh no, child. You don't have the calling."

"But I thought I heard God whisper to me that I was supposed to be a priest."

"No. That wasn't God. It was something else. Don't worry yourself about this anymore. You just be as good as you can." She stared at the son of Scrapper Jack Hourihan, took in my silence for a few seconds, then added, "Go eat your lunch."

I couldn't help wondering if she knew something about me that I didn't know.

I talked with Sean and God that afternoon on the playground at recess, and I came away with the newfound knowledge that I was not going to be a priest. As I pulled my cloth coat tighter and leaned back against the cold granite for warmth against the frozen February air, God agreed with the good sister that I didn't have to become a priest. I asked Him to help me follow these impossible rules, and He said he would, but that, "I didn't have to be overly worried if I screwed up once in a while." I couldn't tell if that last part was God or me, so I finished my sandwich and played tag for the remainder of the recess.

On the way back inside the school, Sean told me, "You know priests don't get to do adultery."

I looked at him in total astonishment. "You mean everyone else has to?"

"Sure, when we get to be adults. It's one of the benefits of not being a priest."

"Benefits? Who told you that?"

"No one. I figured it out myself."

Well, I thought, if Sean figured it out himself, it probably wasn't true. Around then I stopped listening to Sean.

# PART III
The Sacraments and Prayer

## CHAPTER 21
The Red Coats Are Coming

**MARCH HAD JUST BEGUN, AND** every adult I knew was talking excitedly about some Russian general named Stalin who had just died and about an American general who was the new President of the United States. Even the nuns patrolling the arrival of the buses at school had worn "I LIKE IKE" buttons for months. I was confused how Dwight Eisenhower could be shortened to "Ike." It made no sense. But I was more confused about how everyone liked one guy and hated the other. They had the same job in the same war, didn't they, and they were on the same side, weren't they? Adults were strange, and as I got older, they just got stranger.

After doing dishes one night, we sat on the floor around my mother while she read us a story about a boy who refused to grow up. I was very interested, since I hadn't known that was an option. She read, and we imagined how he came in one night through a window and taught the kids in a family how to fly. It was a magical story at a perfect time in my life. That was the answer. I just won't grow up, then I won't have to deal with war and adultery. A few days later, she told us we were all going to the State Theater, the one the rich people went to instead of the rat-infested Ideal Theater.

"We're going to see Peter Pan. I think you'll like it."

"Holy crap," I thought. "He's real?"

It was no easy task to get seven overly excited children fed, washed, and dressed for the movies, and God only knows how my parents came up with enough money for us all to take a cab to town and pay for us to get into the show. My father pushed open the doors to the inner sanctum. The rows of plush maroon seats extended out from where we stood to the pleats of the brown velvet curtains in the front of the room. Each seat had its own plastic ashtray in the arm. The chairs stretched out before us into the semi-darkness. The air inside was warm and rushed out to greet us with a faint hint of popcorn, butter, and cigarette smoke. A few lights above the curtain lit the room just enough so we could see our way inside.

"What do you think, Jocko?" my father asked me. I couldn't answer. I could hardly breathe.

My practical mother took us about halfway down the center aisle then ushered us into an empty row while my father went for popcorn. As the seats filled up with kids who bought chocolate milk at school and the parents who dropped fives and tens into the poor box, I took stock of how many were in my grade. Danny Mac came in with his parents. His mother waved to mine, and they came to sit in front of us.

I leaned forward and whispered to him, "one, two, three," and we both laughed. We wouldn't be kneeling backwards on our seats tonight, but it was not lost on either of us that, if we had to, it would be much easier with the cushions. Then, just as my father came back with armfuls of popcorn bags, the lights dimmed, and the theater turned so black I couldn't see Danny only a few feet away. Then the curtains squeaked wide.

It was the most enlightening experience I had ever had. Sitting in the blackness of the theater, the screen, as large as the entire side of my house, became alive with light, and music filled my head from every corner of the room, and I heard Wendy and Peter and Michael and John. The people on the screen were the size of the trees behind my house. They forged through the most amazing adventures. It was an experience I never imagined could exist in the same world as I did. I flew with the Darlings over London, through the night sky and across an ocean, far from 197 Purchase Street and out to a place where good is good and bad is bad, where war was a game where no one died, where fights were fair, and the bad guys always lost, a world where faeries were real, just like on the Isle of Mann. You never had to grow up, and when someone stole someone from you, they gave them back. All my pre-school expectations of life came back to me as real, and once again I embraced the old ways.

I had seen my first movie in a theater. I was happy, but because of the immenseness of its world, I left feeling smaller than I ever had felt. It was as if I hadn't known anything before Peter Pan. I slid into bed that night and closed my eyes.

"Straight on 'til morning."

## What Is a Sacrament?

School that Monday did nothing to change my comfortable lack of self-confidence.

"What is a sacrament, children?" Sister asked, just after we had turned from kneeling backwards on our chairs and had returned to the relative comfort of sitting.

"Sst, Sst, Sst!" The sibilant call for attention echoed down the spit-and-polished walls of the school, filtering out from each room and then joining with each other stream of "Sst" coming from each other room, and then it cascaded down the stairs and ran amuck in the halls of St. Mary's like a runaway herd of snakes.

"Sst, Sst," being the shortened form of "Sister," and each child who believed he or she had the right answer to a question raised a right hand and began the plea for Sister's attention. "Sst, Sst, Sst."

Jake and I would sometimes raise our hands and do our impression of this foolishness even when we had no idea what the question was, let alone the answer. That was the case this time. "Sst, Sst, Sst." I laughed and waved my arm in the air, and she called on me.

"Uh…" I knew better than to say, "I don't know what you are talking about," so I looked around me, and Kathy Gavin mouthed the word "*Sacrament*."

"Oh, yes, Sister, it is something the priest gives us to make us nicer."

"Go stand in the corner, Mr. Hourihan."

"Miss Gavin?"

"A sacrament is an outward sign instituted by Christ to give grace, Sister."

"That is correct."

I wasn't upset at being sent to the corner again. I was just happy that the prettiest girl in class had tried to help me out. So, before I made it out of my chair, I made a face acknowledging that fact to Jake. He raised his eyebrow again, and we laughed.

Sister didn't even say anything this time. She just pointed to the corner, which made Jake laugh even more, but he was pretty much a silent laugher so he got away with it. When I laughed, it was right out loud. I had just been sent to the corner while I was already headed for the corner. It must have been some kind of record.

"How many sacraments are there?"

I raised my hand, standing in the corner, facing the picture of the Blessed Virgin Mary in the back of the room and said, "Sst, Sst, Sst." I knew the answer. I had studied, but as I expected, she didn't call on me.

"There are seven sacraments: Baptism, Confirmation, Holy Eucharist, Penance, Anointing of the Sick, Holy Orders, and Matrimony."

It was Mulchahy. I knew the voice. I didn't have to turn around. His father had donated a place to the church to be used each spring for a fundraising carnival. Donald was said to have "the calling," but Jake and I doubted it. He cheated on the tests in religion class, for one thing. I figured that was pretty damning.

"From whom do the sacraments receive their power to give grace?"

"The sacraments receive their power to give grace from God, through the merits of Jesus Christ," Mulchahy parroted.

The entitled little creep just kept answering question after question without even being called on, and Sister was letting it happen. She couldn't see from her desk what I could see from my vantage point in the punishment corner. Mulchahy was reading from his book that was secretly opened on his lap.

While I struggled with whether I should speak up, the question-and-answer period ended.

"Children, today we are going to have art class."

"It is March, and we all know what happens in March, don't we?"

"Easter," Mulchahy blurted in his most assured voice.

"No... Easter is in April this year. March 17, as most of you know, is St. Patrick's Day. So, let's see, who knows something about St. Patrick and the Irish?"

"Sst, Sst." My hand shot up, but she called on Mulchahy.

"Yes, Donald?"

"He chased all the snakes out of Ireland."

"Okay," she said, obviously expecting something else.

"And they all moved to Boston and became cops," I added, repeating what was common knowledge in my family.

She scowled. "Mr. Hourihan, do you know anything religious about St. Patrick? Go sit down."

"He taught there were three persons in God with the shamrock, like there were three leafs in a shamrock on one stem." I would have been proud of myself if pride hadn't been a sin.

The list was added to by the mostly Irish class. There were the banshees, the blight, the harp, the pipe, the Troubles, the song Danny Boy. There was the wearin' o' the green, and there were the parades in Boston and New York, and of course there were the little people.

"Yes," said Sister, "and we are going to color some leprechauns for art class."

She produced something we had never seen before. The

school had purchased a mimeograph machine with money donated, of course, by the Mulchahy family or the Garrin family. There, being passed out by Danny Mac, were the purple-outlined pictures of a leprechaun with his jaunty hat, his buttoned jacket, and his buckled shoes. Beside him was a pot-o-gold. It was strangely warming that my friend, who was poor like me, got to hand these things out.

God, these pictures smelled good. Then, when I held it up to my face to get a good whiff, I noticed something.

"Yes, Mr. Hourihan?"

"There are supposed to be seven rows of seven buttons, Sister. There's only three buttons here."

"And what makes you think that?"

"My Grandmother's family is from the Isle of Mann where the little people live, along with the Faeries, of course."

"Well." She looked at her own copy of the drawing then said, "Well, there wasn't room for seven times seven buttons, so we'll color this one." She hesitated, "If that is okay with you, of course."

"Okay," I said, satisfied that I had been taken seriously.

But then when I brought my picture, all colored, up to her desk, she laughed softly and self-assuredly.

"Well, Mr. Hourihan, it seems you don't know everything there is to know about the little people. His coat is supposed to be green—like these others." She showed me a handful of the work done by my friends, and strangely enough they all had green coats.

"No, Sister, they're wrong. Some faeries are blue or green. A leprechaun's coat is red."

"And how do you know that, John?" She had stopped laughing and was asking in a kind voice, like an older sister who wasn't pissed at you that day.

"Because my grandmother has a photograph of a real leprechaun, and his coat is red. It was taken on the Isle of Mann where they come from, and of course from Michael O'Cuileannain the historian himself. Peter Pan has a green coat. I guess that's why they all made a mistake."

I didn't know it, but I had ventured onto the very shaky ground between the old ways of Ireland and Christianity, and this Irish-American nun did not want to deal with it in front of a whole class of children who she was supposed to be bringing up Catholic, and most of whom were weaned on Irish mythology. She shuffled my picture into the others and nodded.

"Go ahead and sit down. Red is fine."

When she put them up the next day, they stretched from one side of the top of the black board to the other, and proudly in the middle was my picture with the red coat. I guessed she had looked it up.

# CHAPTER 22
## The Baptism of the Children of God

"NOT AN APPLE," JAKE SAID.

"What do you mean, not an apple? It was an apple. She ate an apple and then made Adam eat it."

Jake and I stood outside the front door to the school. March had turned warm, and the doors stayed closed after lunch until it was time for class. He was trying to tell me his mother had explained to him that Eve didn't eat an apple.

"Not an apple," he said, eating a cookie from his lunch. "Quince."

"Quints?" The only quints I knew of were the Dionne quints, the five Canadian girls in that Three Stooges episode.

"Quints? Are you crazy? She ate the quints?"

"Yup. Le coing."

"Lecoing my foot. Eve didn't eat any five people. That's just crazy."

"People? What are you talking about? A quince is a fruit."

"Never heard of it."

"Of course you haven't, you fool. That's why they tell us it's an apple."

The doors opened, and there stood Sister Mary Patrick, the enforcer nun of the Order of St. Joseph. She rang the huge cow bell, and we all formed our lines in anticipation. The Sousa march began, and we filed into the school. Our line marched directly into the first door on the right, first grade.

One.

Two.

Three.

Today we said a Hail Mary and an Our Father and turned back around for our lessons. Lately, Sister had been saving the Apostle's Creed for the after-lunch prayer. It was longer and gave us a chance to let our food settle.

"What is Baptism, Miss O'Brien?"

"Baptism is the sacrament that gives our souls the new life of sanctifying grace by which we become children of God and heirs of heaven, Sister."

"Very good, Miss O'Brien.

"What sins does Baptism take away, Mr. Hourihan?"

"Baptism takes away original sin and also, actual sin and all the punishment due to them, if the person baptized be guilty of any actual sins and truly sorry for them, Sister."

"Well done… and what are the effects of the character imprinted on the soul by baptism?"

She looked around the room and settled on Jake.

"Mr. Dubois? Jacques?"

He didn't hear her or had forgotten his name wasn't really Jake.

I reached over and shoved him.

"You," I whispered.

He lurched into action. "The effects of the character imprinted on the soul by Baptism are that we become members of the Church, subject to its laws and capable of receiving other sacraments, Sister."

We had learned from Mulchahy. When she finally turned away, we looked at each other and smiled, our books open on our laps. Maybe now we'd get the calling.

Baptism was done before we even knew who we were, and it made it possible for us to get all the other sacraments, sort of like buying an Irish Sweepstakes ticket. "You can't win if you don't play, and you have to buy a ticket to play." At least that's what my father told me, and Baptism let you play.

I had once gotten a dollar for my birthday from my Aunt Pamela, and when my father found out he said, "You give me that dollar, and I'll turn it into more money than you ever saw. I'll buy you a number in the Irish Sweepstakes. You can't win if you don't play."

A few weeks later I asked him where my money was, and he said, "Oh, you mean your dollar? You lost it. You shouldn't gamble."

I was devastated. A dollar was a lot of money, more than I had ever had before, and now I had nothing. And it left me wondering if I had been gambling on Baptism alone to get me to heaven.

## Family Education

It was a Tuesday. It was fifty degrees and sunny, with a breeze that made it a little chilly when we made our way to the buses to go home. It was St. Patty's Day, and it had been a green day at school with stories of shamrocks and pictures of little people, Irish songs in music class, The Saint himself, and Milford's Irish round tower, the only real round tower in the country according to every Irish descendent in town. They said Father Cuddihy himself brought it over, stone by stone, from County Cork. We had some time left after Sister ended music class, and she smiled and asked us from her desk, "Does anyone know any religious jokes?"

It seemed a strange request, but I raised my hand because I had heard a religious joke at my grandmother's house only last weekend.

"Yes, Mr. Hourihan."

"There were these two bums," I started, but she broke in.

"Hobos, call them hobos."

"There were these two hobos, and they were hungry, so

one says, 'let's go to the rectory and get some food.' And the other one laughs and says, 'You don't get food at a rectory.' But when they get there, the one bum… hobo… goes in and comes out with a sandwich and a bottle of orangeade. The other hobo asks him how he got it, and he says, 'I told them my uncle was a priest, and he told me if I was ever hungry, I should go to the rectory and tell them.' So, the second bum goes in, and pretty soon he gets thrown out with no food and no drink, and the other guy asks him why, and he says, 'I don't know. I thought I might get more than a sandwich if I added to the story, so I told him my father was a priest and my mother was a nun.'"

Sister bolted from her chair. "That's enough, who told you that?"

I was dumbfounded; everyone at Grammy's had laughed. I looked around the room and everyone was frozen in horror. "My Uncle Norman, why?"

"Why do you think that is funny?" She seemed beside herself in anger, and I thought nuns weren't supposed to get angry.

"Because nuns and priests can't get married, so that's funny, right?"

The bell rang, and mercifully it was time to get in line for the buses. When I got off the bus, went in the house, and told my mother what had happened, she laughed even harder than they had at Grammy's, so I was doubly confused. Later, I waited at the window for dad to come home from the shop. When the black coupe stopped at the top of the driveway, I ran out to meet him, and we sat on the stone wall for a few minutes until the chill drove us into the barn. On the way, he told me not to worry about the joke, and we each picked up a handful of egg-sized rocks. At the door to the barn, we stopped.

"You first," he said.

I fired my first rock, and it thudded on the wooden back wall of the barn just to the right of the white metal sign.

"Don't aim. Just look at where you want to hit, and then just fire it," he told me. Then he showed me, and his rock clanged off the metal sign as it always did.

My second rock hit the sign, and he patted me on the back.

"What does it mean?" I asked.

"What?"

"That sign."

In front of us was a one-by-two-foot white metal sign that my father said he had ripped from the front of the Draper building in Hopedale, the next town over. In big black letters on a white background it said, "IRISH NEED NOT APPLY." He hopped up on the work bench that ran from front to back of the barn, and I took my place on a wooden crate opposite him.

"Well, Jocko, it wasn't but a few years ago that the businesses around here didn't want to hire Irish people. So, they told us not even to apply for a job, because that would be a waste of time and paper. I took this one from a place that found out I was Irish and fired me."

"Didn't they know? I mean, everyone knows Hourihan is Irish."

"Well, they weren't too bright. I used a different name when I applied. It seems the only way they can tell you are Irish is by your name and your brogue. All we had to do was lose the brogue and change the name."

"Why didn't they want to hire us?"

"I don't know. I think they didn't want us moving out of the cities. They didn't want us moving up in life."

"Did we move out of the city?"

"Well, I guess we did. We came from Worcester, and my father came from New York."

I sat for a while and thought. He fired another stone at the sign.

Then I asked him something that had been hanging around in my mind since I first heard it. "Who are the Dead Rabbits? You know, like Grampy said."

He looked down at me for more than a few seconds, and I watched the dust float in the afternoon sunbeam that was coming through the window behind him.

"Well, when your Grampy came over here from Ireland, he landed in New York City and right away fell into some bad luck. He was beaten by a policeman."

"Did he do something wrong?"

"No. He says that day he was just walking down the street looking for a place to stay, and the copper stops him and asks his name, and when he says Cornelius Hourihane, he gets paddy whacked and taken in. Some ancient family problems from the old country, we guessed. They beat him up pretty thorough, then let him go with a warning, but he was now convinced he needed to do something to get himself protected from the cops and other thugs on the street, so he joined this group of very feared men called the Dead Rabbits."

I sat quietly while he lit a cigarette. He inhaled the smoke then blew it out in a flourish.

"They were a gang. At the time when he joined, they were taken over by a different group and were most often called something else, but some of the older men in the new gang still called themselves Dead Rabbits. By that time, they had lost most of their clout. About forty years before, they had been the toughest group of men, women, and boys in the city, even fought a huge battle in '57 that included a whole bunch of gangs, and the riot brought in city and state cops. But pretty much when he joined up, they were spending their time protecting each other from the cops and settling disputes between unions and bosses. The men who still called themselves Dead Rabbits were his friends. They protected him as a twenty-two-year-old boy, so that is who he is remembering when he gives that toast."

"Can we join them?"

"No. They aren't around anymore, and besides, they were damn sure a violent bunch of boys. They were mostly criminals… but they protected Grampy when he was a boy in a new country, so he remembers them as his saviors."

"Like Jesus?"

"Sure, like Jesus."

He fired his last rock, hit the sign, and laughed.

"Besides, we don't need protecting. We're Irish, and the Irish are born fighters." He winked down at me. "And the Hourihans are called the 'descendants of the warrior.' We protected the high kings and their families. Don't you forget that."

"I won't," I said with the firm knowledge in my head that I was one of the smallest kids in my grade, including most of the girls, and I figured if there was a high king, he was in dire need of a bigger warrior.

"What about Uncle Frankie?"

He looked down at me, squinting his eyes. "What about Uncle Frankie?" he repeated.

"Did he really kill some guy for calling him an IRA baby killer?"

"Who told you that?"

"Sean."

He nodded in understanding, and then he sat for a while, thinking.

"Well," he said finally, "I wasn't with him, but I doubt if he was protecting the honor of the Irish Republican Army. The IRA didn't even begin until our family had left Ireland, but the rest is true. It was an accident, and the other guy started the fight."

He snuffed out his cigarette on the bench and lit another one.

"I suppose you are old enough to know." He took a sidelong look out the open barn door as if he was looking to make sure we were alone.

"Jocko…" Again, he stalled. He jumped off the bench to the floor and began to walk back and forth in front of me.

"There was something I remember from a time when I was just a bit older than you are now. It seems a young man, really a boy, became involved in the politics of Ireland, and he and some friends were convinced by some older men, a couple of right gurriers to be true, into doing some mighty nasty things on their behalf." He looked at me again to see if I was listening. "The boy got caught." Now he came and sat cross legged on the floor in front of my crate. "He was faced with jail until he was too old to have children… or he could turn in the men who put him up to it."

"He ratted!?" I couldn't believe it. I had always been taught, even by the man I was now talking to, that there was nothing lower than a stool pigeon.

"They were cowardly men who convinced trusting boys to do their dirty work. If he hadn't given them up, he'd be in jail to this very day. He never would have gotten to come to America, and none of us would be here. He was your Grampy.

"The men came after him from time to time; right here to the United States. Sometimes your grandfather had to sleep in the kitchen, lying across the doorway with a shotgun. The last time, I was just a boy, and we were living in Northbridge. When we heard about how they had found him, he sent out a few of his older sons to take care of it."

He meaningfully snuffed out his cigarette on the floor.

"It was the last time anyone came to get your Grampy."

He smiled as he said, "We better get inside for dinner, whadya think?"

I agreed, and we started into the house.

"Oh, by the way, we don't have to tell your mother about the IRA and the Dead Rabbits, right?"

"Right." The older I got, the more things I knew that I couldn't tell my mother.

Over dinner, my mother asked what we had been talking about. My father's face froze, expecting me to rat on him about our family's own original sin, but he melted when I said, "How our family used to be warriors."

"Right," my father echoed. "Champions of the high king and his family."

"Like Sir Lancelot?" I asked, remembering a book my mother had read us.

"No," Scrapper answered. "He was English."

Sweet Genevieve chimed in immediately, "No. He was French, so on my side, Johnny is right. Like Lancelot." She smiled the smile of victory right across the table at my proud Irish father. As I waded silently into my meatloaf, dandelion greens, and mashed potatoes, I figured, if my mother was French and Scottish and my father was Irish, and all their children were Irish, French and Scottish, maybe Sean was right. How else would we become a combination of the two people?

After dinner, I went outside to ponder the future dilemma of what exactly Sean had been talking about, and what the heck was a beaver?

# CHAPTER 23
Some Sacraments Are for Now, Some for Later

**THE SUN IN APRIL LOOKED** the same as it had all winter as it rose across the field behind the barn, but now it felt warmer. The snow had all melted away, and the still-brown grass began to rise from its flattened state. We were in those bittersweet days during the approach to the rebirths of Easter and Spring. Religion and reality.

Penance would be the next sacrament we would learn about, and then Holy Communion, but that wouldn't come until next year in second grade. After practicing how to make a good confession, I had a strong idea of what penance was going to be like.

I had already been told by a nun that I would not be getting

## Baltimore Catechism: Clean Slate (Fall and Rise of a Catholic Boy)

Holy Orders anytime soon, since I didn't have "the calling." Confirmation was far in the distant era of the teen years, and Matrimony was only for adults, and even then they would have to have adultery, so I pushed that off into the black recesses of my brain. Then of course came Extreme Unction, the sacrament that nobody wanted because it meant you were going to die. But for now, we were learning about how to confess our sins to the priest so we might receive the body and blood of Christ next year at our First Holy Communion. Since the actual occurrence would be so far off, we got to practice on a nun, or in my case on Miss Granell. Miss Granell was one of those ambiguous human beings who settled somewhere between reality and religion. She was a "lay teacher" in a parochial school.

I didn't know much about penance at the outset of the day when we began to learn how to confess our sins, and I was shocked to know that I would be given penance a year before I even had to confess for real, and not even by a priest. Miss Granell stepped into the room and took Sister Thomas Joseph's place in the front.

"My name is Miss Granell." She wrote it on the board, and I smiled, knowing that according to my old man she had left a letter off. My father for some reason didn't get along with her and sometimes would talk about her at home, questioning why she should even be teaching at the school without her being a nun. A lot of people felt the same way, but my father in his Irishness had a strange idea of why she shouldn't be where she was.

She turned back from the board and faced us with a somber look.

"Sister isn't feeling well, so I will fill in for her today."

Miss Granell was tall and thin with red hair. Her face was soft and freckled and not unpleasant, but she never seemed to smile. I sat in my chair, satisfied that I knew something about her the others didn't.

"So," she continued, "how should we begin our confession?"

In unison we chanted, "We should begin our confession in this manner: Entering the confessional, we kneel, and making the sign of the cross we say to the priest: 'Bless me, Father.'"

We then went on to regurgitate how we should tell if we had committed any mortal sins, like murder, or missing Mass on Sunday. Jake and I practiced making up sins in case we had no mortal sins to confess, and then we found out it was okay to bring up old sins that you are still sorry for if you hadn't sinned that week. Cousin Sean told me this was so the priest would have something to absolve, "otherwise he'd be out of a job." He laughed. I figured he had heard it from his old man.

Miss Granell even gave us a "confession trick" to use.

"When you don't remember how many of each sin you committed, but you don't want to tell a lie, you just say 'five or six' or 'nine or ten' or something close." She was very proud of this, and it showed in her pursed lips and her spin back toward the front of the room. Nevertheless, we were very appreciative of her advice from her own confessional experience. I thought, nine or ten? Damn, this girl could sin. Nine or ten of the same sin in a week?

"Class, how should we end our confession?" she said as she spun back around to face us.

"We should end our confession by saying: 'I am sorry for these and all the sins of my past life, especially for...'" And then we were told it is well to tell one or several of the sins which we have previously confessed and for which we would be particularly sorry. Jake and I chose our made-up sin from the past that we would be particularly sorry for if it ever came to that. I chose disrespecting my parents, and Jake chose adultery.

In front of the room, Miss Granell was plummeting into today's lesson.

"What is prayer?"

"Prayer is the lifting up of our minds and hearts to God," we said in unison.

We learned that we could pray for blessings for ourselves, our families, and our friends and enemies, and if nothing happened, it was because God said, "No." The part I liked the most was we could make up our own prayers, which is what I had been doing since I prayed for a fireplace just like Spike's but didn't get it. God must have thought cold was good for me.

I raised my hand. "Miss Granell, may I go to the basement?"

Basement was a euphemism for bathroom, which was a word one didn't say in public, like "pregnant" or "toilet."

"No, not now. Lunch isn't that far away."

I sat, astonished that I wasn't allowed to go to the boys' room. It wasn't that I had to go so bad, but I was just a bit put out that someone who wasn't even a nun could tell me when I could or couldn't relieve myself. I stood up, and with all my classmates' eyes wide in horror, I walked down the aisle and left the room. While the young woman stared helplessly, I carefully closed the door behind me. I descended the back stairs into the bowels of the building and went to the boys' room. I had surprised even myself. When I returned from "the basement," climbing freely up the heavy and wide wooden staircase, and was approaching the classroom, I stopped in sheer fright. My heart jumped, my eyes watered, and I nearly had to go again. Standing in front of the door was Sister Mary Patrick, and she was looking directly at me. Her stare drew me like a tractor beam from a Buck Rogers comic to a spot a few feet in front of her, and she looked down at me with a practiced stern face.

"Did Miss Granell tell you not to go to the basement?"

"Yes, Sst." I would have said Sister, but I was too scared.

"And you went anyway?"

"Yes, Sst."

I thought it was possible that I might "Yes, Sister" my way out of any penance.

"Do you think that was the right thing to do?"

"Yes, Sst."

"What?"

"I had to pee."

"You were told not to go, and don't say pee, say number one or number two."

"I tried, but it didn't work. I still had to go number," I thought for a few seconds. I had no idea which number was which but eventually I asked, "one?"

"Yes, one, but Miss Granell told you not to go at all."

"Sister, she doesn't even belong here. She isn't even Irish. Her name is really Granelli. She belongs at Sacred Heart."

"Who told you that?" Her head cocked itself to the side like a dog does when it is about to bite you.

"My father." I figured that should hold some weight.

She shook my head by the hair. I looked sideways up at her in hopes I could find a way out of her grasp. I looked at her reddening face. Wait a minute, she was laughing, but I was still being punished. In situations where I felt helpless, I did the same thing I always did. I prayed a made-up prayer. "Jesus, please make this crazy nun let go of my head."

Miraculously, she let go of my hair, stepped back, pointed silently to the room. I returned to my seat, leaving her in the hall. A few moments later, I heard a gaggle of nuns laughing on the other side of the door. I had never been so confused. I was being punished, and they thought it was funny. Was she happy that I was being punished or was something else making them laugh?

When I told my mother that afternoon, she laughed too. I couldn't understand how I got pulled by the hair and no one cared. They even found it funny. It seemed to me that, while doing penance was making me feel bad, it was also making some other people feel really good about themselves, even enough to make them laugh. Then things got worse. On Good Friday, the whole school emptied around two o'clock, and each teacher walked her class out of the school, up Winter Street, and into the church to hear the visiting priest say the Stations of the Cross. Miss Granell was still filling in for Sister Thomas Joseph, who we heard was really sick. As luck had it, I was the first pupil into the pew, and got stuck up against the wall, and there were about fifteen kids between myself and Miss Granell, who sat at the very first seat in the row. She had the same effect on me that she had always had since the day when she had said, "No."

When someone tells you that you are not allowed to go to the bathroom, whenever you see them again you want to go. Well, at least that's how she affected me. Seeing her made me want to pee. Sean said she had "scared the piss out of me." Right now, at the end of this pew, I had to go. I didn't dare ask her to leave when we had only gotten to the second station where Jesus had just begun to carry his cross. I figured if Jesus could carry His cross, I could hold it until the end. But by the fourth station where Jesus met his mother, my knee was jumping uncontrollably. I looked to the end of the row where the stern red-headed teacher must have felt my stare and bent forward and looked right down the row at me. I turned back to watch the priest on his journey around the pictures on the walls of the church. At the eighth station where Jesus meets the women of Jerusalem, I prayed to God that I wouldn't have to pee. He said, "No." I could hold it no longer. I could climb over the back of the pew, but she would just take one step backward and stop me, and I couldn't just get up and leave because my way was blocked by fifteen or so kids and Granelli.

As Father sang in his monotone about the women of Jerusalem, I knelt up straight and just relaxed. The priest was visiting from some country that the missions paid for, and I could hardly understand a thing he was saying. It had been the same last Sunday when he read the gospel. I understood nothing except at the end when he said, "Da Gospel, according to Mark."

At the end of the Stations of the Cross, everyone stood in unison and turned toward Miss Granell. She stood and watched us all walk toward her, me with my books held discretely in front of myself. She never saw the wet spot on the front of my pants, and she never saw the puddle that was left at the end of the pew. I carried my books in front of me back down to the buses and home, where I went immediately to my room and changed. No one would ever know, except me and God, and maybe whoever cleaned the church.

After dinner, I walked by myself out the back door of my home and, avoiding dish duty, crossed the side yard between the barn and the house. I sat on the stone wall on the other side of the driveway and watched Spike's dog, Prince, playing in Gonhue's field. I couldn't believe what had happened, how I had been so helpless against the power of one person who had been put in charge of me for no good reason. It occurred to me that when we walked in the woods, we peed wherever we wanted. At home, if the toilet wasn't working we just went out behind the barn, but at the school, where there were about a dozen urinals right in the basement and about as many in the church, you had to ask someone if you could have permission to go, and then people had the right to say, "No." This made no sense to me at all. Somehow, certain people got themselves put in charge of when and where we got to do probably the most humanly natural thing in the world. How could this have anything to do with being good? How could it have anything to do with religion? I decided that from then on, I would go to the bathroom every time I got a chance, whether or not I had to go.

# CHAPTER 24
Putting Prayer to Use

**THAT SATURDAY MORNING, I SAT** in the dirt in the yard, with my back against my rock, next to the barn in the natural beauty of spring on Purchase Street, with the satisfying knowledge that I could sit when I wanted, run when I wanted, throw stones if I wanted, and go take a leak behind the barn any time I wanted, and I would no longer wait for anyone's permission. It was Saturday, the only natural day left in the week.

Sunday was Easter, I loved the story of Easter, and the nuns loved to tell it. Sister Superior came in and read to us on Good Friday. We'd colored Easter lilies, and the cross, and then on Sunday we would go to the most ornate Mass of the year.

But this was Saturday; one of those wonderful days that had no name, no schedule, no unnatural significance. I had gotten up just after sunrise and took a box of Kix with me to Linda's house and sat on the swings with her. It was only fifty degrees, but after a cruel winter fifty is warm enough, and we let the sun beat down on us as we swung on the chain-hung swings eating sugared cereal from the box.

Linda looked up suddenly and squinted at a scream that came from above the field between us and the tree line. I listened as a second, higher-pitched squeal came again, and I pointed to a place about halfway across the field, out past the chicken coops. We both knew the meaning of a hawk's scream when he had found food and the sound of a chipmunk fighting for its natural life. Being children of nature, we knew a lot of things such as this. In order to know which berries to eat, we had to know which ones were poisonous and which ones were not. We knew chickens' eggs, if left in the nest, hatched into chickens, and those we ate never had a life. We knew rabbits made good pets and good stew. We knew that the flowers that died in fall were reborn in the spring, but not humans, and we knew the green shoots only an inch high next to the house would produce flowers first because of the proximity to the warmth of Linda's home. We knew how lucky we were to have been born Americans, the land of the free and the home of the brave, and we knew we were a part of the only true religion in the world. It was spring, and everything was coming back to life, except maybe that chipmunk. And we knew that we accepted each other for exactly who we were. It was a beautiful day, warm and comfortable, swinging in the back yard next to the old and rusting Essex with a friend; no lessons to learn, no punishments, no sacraments, no prayers, no commandments, no traditions. There weren't any sins to confess, no evil inclinations. It was a six-year-old's heaven.

The next day was Easter. The church was brilliant with white and yellow cut lilies lining the side walls. Everyone was dressed up, as if there were never to be another day in this life. There was the smell of burning palms from Palm Sunday the week before, still hovering inches from the floor under the benches and in the pockets in the seatbacks in front of us, and there were huge yellowish candles and purple irises on the altar. The nuns smiled through the whole Mass, and the priest couldn't stop himself from saying "hallelujah" a ton of times in his sermon.

We had woken to baskets of jelly beans, yellow marshmallow chicks, soft candy peanuts, and one full-sized candy bar in a basket of fake multicolored plastic hay. We were primed for an Easter egg hunt at Grammy's, and of course, I got in trouble for a question in her living room after Mass.

"It doesn't make any sense," I told my cousin Katey.

I liked Katey. She was a sweet and shy girl with long blonde hair and Hourihan blue eyes, and she was smarter than most of my cousins and classmates.

"What doesn't make sense?" she asked. My Aunt Kathleen was sitting in the Morgan chair just above the two of us who were squatted on the rug. At Katey's question, my aunt began to listen more closely. We were sitting on the floor in front of her, waiting for candy and colored eggs to be brought out from the brown bags in the kitchen that we had pretended not to notice.

"Sister said on the third day He arose again from the dead."
"So?"
"So, He died Friday afternoon."
"So what?"
"Well, Saturday afternoon would be one day, right?"
"Right."
"And Sunday afternoon would be two days, right?"

Aunt Kathleen slapped me in the head from behind. "One more word and it's the back o' me hand to ya."

I didn't look up, just locked eyes with Katey, smiled, and said, "Yes, Sister." It could have been by mistake, but mistake or not, it awarded me another slap. Katey laughed a bit, but she hid it well and escaped any smacking. I laughed too. It hadn't hurt. It had occurred to me that if I was going to be Catholic, there were just some things you didn't ask. At least not in front of Aunt Kathleen.

Katey and I hurried off to the kitchen where the individual baskets for each of the cousins had been brought out and now covered the whole table. We started looking for our own, when Grammy said in an unnaturally soft and loving voice, "Not yet. After you eat."

It was hard to be disappointed at such a perfect time;

the smell of palms and Easter ham, the piety of the Mass, and the sun-drenched walk across town, the warmth of family, marshmallow chicks, Mary Janes, squirrels, caramels, NECCO wafers, and Jesus came back from the dead. What a great day, except for one thing. Dennis had gotten sick and was in the hospital with pneumonia. He couldn't breathe. I took some time at Mass to pray for him.

Grammy had a cross that opened hanging on the wall that would serve for what she called Extreme Unction. She was telling my mother she should take it home with us, "For poor young Dennis." The nuns called it "anointing the sick," but we all knew it was for people who weren't sick but next to death. She opened the front of the cross and showed my mother the bottle of oil inside and the bottle of Holy Water.

Mom took it, thanked her, and the second we were outside she tossed it into the neighbor's yard behind the shrubs. "Damn fool. He's sick, not dying," she said as she slammed the door of Uncle Con's car.

## The Missions

Most of the rest of first grade was spent in learning, not religious rules, but the rules of the Catholic school, and at home I was to learn more about how the Irish were born to fight.

"Children," Sister Superior began, "We here in the United

States are very lucky indeed. We are allowed to practice our faith, we are allowed to be anything we want to be, we have a say in what our government does, and we have a roof over our heads and food in our bellies… but that is not the way it is all over the world."

I made my face at Jake, the one where I squinted my one visible eye and sneered my lip, the face that said, "What the hell is she talking about?"

"It is our duty as Catholics to help the poor. Father Pietro is here from South America, from a village that is rife with hunger and illness and demons. The children there have little hope. They need our help, and how do we help them?"

"The money we give to the missions, Sister." It was Kathy who had answered without raising her hand. I was impressed. Of course, we boys were all impressed with Kathy anyway, no matter what she did.

"That's correct, Miss Gavin. The money we give to the missions. So, from now on, every day we will be collecting money from all of us to give to Father Pietro when he leaves at the end of the month to return to his village.

"Oh, and children, that doesn't mean that we can forget about the Bishop's Relief Fund that we collect for each Friday. That is something entirely different."

I knew, from listening at the pantry wall, that my family had very little money to spare, especially now with Dennis in the hospital, so I made my own decision that I wouldn't tell them about this at all. Instead, I would just split my milk money between the two. I got three cents a day for milk, which gave me fifteen cents a week; five cents to the Bishop and two cents a day to the missions. I didn't much like the milk anyway. When I told Jake about it at recess, he decided to do that too. Problem solved. Jake and I also spoke about how our classes were allowed to go down to the Italian Catholic school, Sacred Heart, on Wednesdays for spaghetti and meatballs with Italian bread and Jell-O.

"I guess we are sort of their mission." Jake smiled, but it left me wondering why we weren't all going to the same school.

## On the Home Front

Something much more interesting was being taught at home during this spring thaw. It was happening in the barn.

"Okay, Jocko," my old man said, as if what he was about to teach me was the most important thing a boy could learn. "Spread your feet like this." He showed me. "Okay, bend your knees, kind of sit down into it, like this."

I did what he told me.

"Now, this is a jab, like this." He thrust out his left fist, turning over the hand part as he snapped it out. "Go ahead, do it." He showed me again. I snapped it out several times.

"No, no, no, pull your chin in against your chest. That's it. Snap out that jab! Good. Now, step a half step forward and with the other hand, do this… that's a hook."

I tried it.

"There you go, Jocko, you're a natural. Now, jab, jab, hook. Go ahead, do it!" He watched as I did it over and over. *Jab, jab, hook; jab, jab hook.*

"There you go," he said, smiling with pride. "That's your first combination."

I practiced it some more, and after a while he said, "Okay, now stick your face right up there. Stand over your lead leg, jab jab, and when he swings at your face, you rock back and then slide in like this." He slid his back foot up a bit then stepped in with his lead foot and let go a powerful right hook into the air. "Set yourself when you throw the hook. Jab jab... hook. Beautiful! You may yet be a relative of John L himself." I knew he meant that the Sullivans were only a few generations back into the Hourihan line, my grandfather's mother having been a Sullivan. When we were done with the day's pugilistic lessons, we sat in our seats. My father sat on the bench, me on the crate, and he told of the Kilmichael Ambush. Dan and Jack Hourihan, relatives of my father, in November of 1920, took on the Brit special forces, and "beat them to a right pulp" in a bog called Kilmichael. "It was the only time the IRA ever totally bested the British Special Forces."

"Is that good?" I asked.

"Yes, it is good. Downright good. We don't like the British all that much."

"Why not?"

"They took our country. They starved us out. They took our land and gave it to their own people, and they hate the Catholics, which is what we are, so we hate them right back."

To this day, it was the best description I ever heard of "The Troubles" in Ireland.

"Let's go get some supper, and I don't think we are needing to tell your mother about the ambush or the combination, right?"

"Right."

"Jab, jab, hook, right?"

"Right."

## CHAPTER 25
Winston Crake Spit at My Friend

**AFTER EASTER, WE RETURNED TO** school and learned about how the bishop would be visiting us that week. It was a big thing, I guess.

At recess, I was hovering on the border between the girls' side and the boys' side of the schoolyard and talking with Elaine. Elaine, Laurie, and Pansy were the children of friends of my mother, and I had known them my whole life. They were my friends, too. They were Irish and French. They were nearly family. A commotion behind me deep into the boys' side dissolved the division between the genders, and we all moved toward the source.

Little Billy Barry was being held by the coat collar by the much larger Winston Crake. I couldn't abide this. I wasn't much bigger than Barry, but I didn't like Crake from when I first saw him, and when he spit at Barry I spoke up.

"Let go of him!" I shouted from the edge of the circle of classmates. Crake looked toward me, but he wasn't sure who had said it.

"Me," I said. "I said it. Let him go!"

Crake was a tall, dark-haired, lanky boy with a rich kid's leather coat, a very white face, and glasses nearly as thick as mine.

"What's it to you?"

"I don't much like the feckin' British," I said. I might have even had a bit of a brogue like my father sometimes did.

He was stunned. At six years old, he probably had never been told that the Irish and the English weren't supposed to get along. I knew better, since it had come from my father. He looked hesitant, but nonetheless, it was going to happen. We squared off; I took off my glasses, spread my legs, and sat into the stance, my face high up over my lead foot, my chin tucked into my chest.

"Take off your glasses," I said. It was only fair.

"No," he said to my surprise, and I realized he probably couldn't see without them.

"Someone hold his glasses for him," I said to the crowd that was now circled around the two of us.

Elaine stepped in. "I'll hold them," she offered and reached out to Crake.

"No," he said, pushing her hand away.

Jab, jab, hook. I hit him hard, stepped into it, then stepped back, set myself forward over my lead foot and jabbed at him again. He saw his opening and lunged forward to throw a wild right at my head. Following instructions, I shifted my body back over my back leg, then as his fist flew by my face I shuffled forward, threw the hook, and he was no longer wearing glasses. They skittled across the asphalt schoolyard, and his nose gushed blood from its flattened position on his right cheek. The fight was over. Crake stumbled toward old Sister Francis Elizabeth who was on schoolyard duty today and hadn't seen a thing. She was leading him toward the basement of the school where she might stop the bleeding. Luckily for me, someone had told him about not being a rat. He told Sister he had fallen down playing "caught, caught, free, free."

I had won. I had done everything my father had told me, but it felt wrong. I couldn't get the vision of Winnie's bloody face out of my head. True, I was protecting someone smaller than me, but only sort of. Most of my head had this English/Irish thing going on. I wanted to do what my father had taught me as much as I wanted to do what my religion had taught me, and I found it was impossible. Sometimes no matter how right you are, you're wrong.

The nuns had become caught up in the bishop's visit that afternoon and forgot to get to the bottom of the bloody nose incident. I spent the entire bus ride home praying the Our Father over and over again. I guess it was because I knew that what I had done was wrong, and I vowed to apologize to Crake when I got a chance, but the chance never came. I guess it was the beginnings of my own inclination to evil. The stark difference between the rules of my religion and the rules of life became clearer to me after that fight than they had ever been. I became more convinced than ever that I was supposed to try my best to go by the laws of God rather than those of Scrapper Jack.

It was my Epiphany.

# CHAPTER 26
A June Descent into Enlightenment

**IT WASN'T MY FAULT.**

The beginning of June brought unseasonably warm weather, and my sister Diane, who was in charge for the day, brought me to the wall, a place that was made of granite blocks deep in the woods by the quarry hole. It was a place where my father had told me never to go, but he had made one mistake. He had pointed out the path and told me, "Never go beyond the brook," but in hot weather the brook had dried up so my boundaries were erased.

There before me, rising into the perfectly blue sky, was a cascade of large quarry blocks of black and gray rock that were piled three times the height of my house. Each block was just a bit taller than my head and two or three times as long as my body, and hundreds of them were stacked one on top of another to the height of a castle. The wall was as wide as the church, but it wasn't the same pink color. We walked around to the left of the wall and up a short pine-needle-covered hill to a large, flat rock the size of our first-grade classroom. We stood and looked out at a sight usually only seen in mid-summer.

A group of about a dozen or so teenagers were there today. Some were climbing to the top, since they could step from one block to the next without stretching. Others stood unafraid at the top, looking down at the water fifty feet below. Still others were already in the water, splashing and laughing together. It was my first encounter with "the Purchase Street Quarry." It was said to be so deep that there were cars at the bottom, and no one could dive far enough to touch them, and it was rumored to be so cold your body could go numb if you didn't get out within minutes of entering the water.

There were dozens of teenage boys and girls, some in shorts and shirts, some undressed to their underwear and jumping off a cliff on the other side that rose high above the surface of the water. They jumped from the cliff, swam across the quarry hole that had, since its closure, been continuously filled with spring water colder than a January bathtub, and then they climbed out onto the flat rock where Diane and I stood. I watched them jump from the rocks over a bush growing on a cliff halfway down and plunge feet first into the water. Half of them came to the surface with at least some of their underclothes half off. They climbed out, pulled on their clothes right in front of us, laughed and scurried back up the pine-needle-covered hill to the precipice and dove off again.

The girls were the most interesting. I had never seen a post-pubescent naked girl before. I watched as a strawberry blonde high schooler flirted at the top of the cliff with two boys. She was trying in vain to retain her white blouse, even though she had already stepped out of her slacks and stood defiantly in her panties and the blouse. The boys were cajoling and reaching delicately for the buttons. Finally, to my surprise, and as an answer to a prayer, she stepped back from them and unbuttoned the blouse, dropped it off, and stood at the precipice in her white underwear, a goddess of the summer fit for the wall of a barbershop. Then she dove head first to the water. She seemed to be under for an eternity, and when she surfaced, she was only twenty feet from the flat rock, swimming with one hand while holding her underwear in the other; all of her underwear.

She stepped out of the water and onto the rock only a dozen feet in front of me, totally naked. She saw my gape, and she smiled. She was totally and exquisitely unclothed. As my eyes traveled from her face down her body, she slowly bent and pulled on her panties, all the while looking at my stunned silence and unblinking eyes with a calm look of acceptance of this awkward situation. She slipped her arms into the straps of her bra, never taking her eyes off me, and almost apologetically reached back with both hands and snapped it on. She smiled to me and trotted off, up the hill, back to the precipice. I watched her run all the way up the hill, marveling at how incredibly beautiful the human body is and lamenting how original sin made us all cover it up. At least now I knew what Sean meant by a beaver.

Diane slapped me on the back of the head. "Close your mouth," she said, and laughed.

Later that afternoon, on my own rock near the barn, I wondered if my father told me how dangerous this area of the woods was, because it was in fact dangerous, or because there were fully grown kids there who were naked. It had been my baptism into the true and only difference between girls and boys, and I instantly understood why Linda's mother didn't want her and me in the woods together. Boys and girls were different. And now I knew *what* got us all tossed out of the Garden of Eden, but I still couldn't figure out *why*.

## CHAPTER 27
A Cold Wind Blowing

**THE END OF SCHOOL AND** the beginning of baseball were near. I would be transferring from one religion to another.

I had been sleeping upstairs on the unfinished wooden floor next to the window for weeks rather than in a crowded bed downstairs. Some nights were still cold, but waking up to a window that overlooked the roof of the barn, the hay field that stretched a half-mile to the wood line, a view of the baseball field across our stone wall, and listening to birds chirping in the outer branches of the trees in our yard was heavenly. That morning was chilly, and when I walked downstairs and into the kitchen with a hot coffee in my hands, my mother's brow knitted. She stood, walked from the table and looked at the stove. It wasn't on. She looked back at the table for coffee, but it wasn't there.

"Where did you get coffee?" she asked, and as an afterthought, "And why are you drinking it?"

"You drink it," I offered.

"But you aren't me. You aren't old enough." She stopped abruptly, and then again she asked, "Where did you get hot coffee?"

"Upstairs."

"How?" Now her attention was fully on me

"I made it with the stove."

As far as she knew there was no stove upstairs, but she had discounted the toy Wolverine tin stove my sisters had gotten from an auction somewhere near last Christmas. The stove, a cup, some wooden matches, some shreds of newspaper, water, and instant coffee grew me up.

She had stopped doing everything but this inquiry now, and she turned to face me.

"What stove?"

I told her.

"That's a toy. It doesn't heat things up." She said it as a question since it obviously had. She was looking at her son, who it seemed had just cut the apron strings and made his own breakfast.

"It does if you light a fire in the oven part and put the cup on top."

She bolted for the back stairs.

"It's out," I said, but she mustn't have believed me.

A few minutes later, she came back down and strangely enough didn't say a word to me. She just went to the stove to make oatmeal and occasionally looked over her shoulder and stared at me. When she was calm enough to speak without knocking my head off, she said, "Don't do that again."

After another few deep breaths, she added, "Go to school."

I trundled up the driveway to wait at the rock for my bus to St. Mary's Central Catholic Grammar School. I was exhilarated.

I stepped off the bus into the front school yard in the middle of the pack and sidled into line behind Jake. School was for all purposes over. All we had left was the Safety Day Parade where we would all parade up Main Street to show everyone driving a car that we had retaken the streets for the summer. Before the parade would begin, we had a few lessons that the nuns dredged up to keep us busy when we weren't taping torn textbook pages or erasing the marks we put in them during the year. I was erasing the clothes I had drawn on Jesus on the cross when Sister Thomas Joseph stood from her desk and stumbled, white faced, toward the door.

"Children be good, I'll be right back," she said as she exited, and I heard her knock on the next classroom door. There was a mumble of the two nuns talking, and then she was helped back out the front door of the building. We were alone for what seemed a longer time than the half hour it was, and then Miss Granell entered the room. I immediately had to pee.

"Sister has been taken to the hospital. She isn't feeling well. We have to finish the Our Father."

She opened *The Baltimore Catechism*. Sister never returned to the school.

Granell took over. "For what do we pray when we say 'and lead us not into temptation,' children?"

"When we say 'and lead us not into temptation,' we pray that God will always give us the grace to overcome the temptations to sin which come to us from the world, the flesh, and the devil, Miss Granelli." I added the missing "i" and she glanced for a second at me, then let it go.

I remembered I hadn't told Jake about what I had seen at the quarry, but as I turned to tell him about it, Miss Granell went on.

"For what do we pray when we say 'but deliver us from evil,' children?"

"When we say 'but deliver us from evil,' we pray that God will always protect us from harm, and especially from harm to our souls, Miss Granell," I said, before adding, "i."

I was pretty sure what I had seen at the quarry had probably done some harm to my soul, but I figured it was worth it. I was not, however, in the mood for this waste of time. It was obvious that the school year was over. We were hours and minutes away from vacation, and I wanted more than anything to tell Jake about the beauty of a naked teenage girl and what I had found out about a beaver. As we finally made it to the school yard at lunch, I blurted it all out.

"She smiled right at me," I told him. "Just like she didn't mind if I was looking."

I described her body to him, the parts we never got to see, and we scanned the schoolyard for a short time at the girls who had been our friends for so many years, then we settled on Mary Margaret, a seventh grader who was already bulging her clothes in ways that we hadn't understood until now.

"I see what you mean," Jake said, and we both looked our fill before the bell rang for us to go in.

We formed our lines, the girls' line first and then the boys. Luckily, we were the first two in the boys' line, and we were flush with the end of the girls' line. I had never realized before that my friends Laurie, Elaine, and Pansy were good looking. I had been awakened by the trip to the wall. I smiled at Elaine, and we started to talk about the Crake fight, when Mulchahy stepped in front of me and shoved me back. He was accustomed to having his own way, because he was rich and a favorite of the nuns.

"Hey," I said, pulling him back and stepping in front of him. "Get in line!"

He shoved ahead of me again, turned, and glared at me. Glaring being his main weapon, learned at home, I guess. Glaring was not one of my weapons. I grabbed his shirt with both hands and pushed him against the granite wall of the building. "Get in line!" I hissed. I was jerked backwards by a very strong force, and I nearly fell to the ground but was held up balanced on my heels. Next, I was spun around and stood in the clutches of Sister Mary Patrick. She looked over my head and asked, "Mr. Mulchahy, are you all right?"

I guess he was, because she now turned her full force back to me. "I have had enough of you," she said in a deeper voice than she usually had. "Come with me."

She pulled me by my jacket collar, shoved me in front of her, and said, "March!" She paraded me along the girls' line, pushing me from time to time to get me to move faster, but she didn't take me into the school. Instead, she pushed me toward the sidewalk on Winter Street and herded me like an animal up past the statue of St. Joseph and to the church. Frightened and angry, I remembered that my mother had told me no one has a right to put their hands on me unless I tell them it's okay. I tried to push her away, but she held tight to my collar.

"You no good Goddamn son-of-a-bitch, get your feckin' hands off me or I'll beat you within an inch of your life!" This always worked for my father, so I figured I'd give it a shot. I pleaded, but she only glared harder.

"You will leave that child alone, do you hear me?" she demanded.

"What?"

"Leave him alone! In the name of Jesus!"

*Damn,* I thought, *they must really like Mulchahy.* I struggled, but she was too strong and wouldn't let go of my collar, and at some point, she began shaking me as if I were one of my sisters' Raggedy Anne dolls. The sidewalk was wet from an earlier rain, and as she pushed me along, I kept slipping. When I fell, she picked me up by my belt and dragged me to my feet.

"Move!" she demanded.

I had no idea what was happening. I mean, Mulchahy started the fight, and where was he? At the entry to the church, she let go of me for a second and pulled open the door. Then she dragged me inside. "I have had enough of this," she said, spinning me toward her and bending to look directly into my soul.

"Get inside!" she said as we pushed through the second set of doors and into the main expanse of the church. She dragged me down the center aisle, never even stopping for me to anoint myself with holy water.

"Father?" she shouted, and it echoed off the walls of the spacious church. "Father, are you here?"

Her calls rattled through the church in an angry insistence, and the air smelled stale and empty and cold. I brushed a fly from my face as the visiting priest stepped from the sacristy to the left of the altar. He was wearing the black pants and jacket and collar of a Catholic priest.

"Yes?" he questioned.

It was "da gospel according to Mark" guy.

"Sit here!" she said and pushed me down into a pew only a few from the front.

The two of them spoke in hushed voices. I heard, "hair falling out, weight loss, black teeth." I was becoming seriously frightened and looked around the church for the familiar face of Father Carbary. He was nowhere in sight. "Foul language and blasphemy," she said, and then she looked at me while still talking to him and said, "And he is exceedingly strong." She held out her arm to show him the red mark at her wrist where I had grabbed her to try to free myself on the "walk" from the school. "And he soiled the church during the Stations of the Cross."

Now I knew who had cleaned the church, and I smiled a little to myself.

He nodded and turned on his heel and went back into the sacristy. She returned and stood over me. "I know it's not your fault, John," she said. "Can you hear me?"

How the hell could I not hear her? She was only inches from my face. This confused me even more. If it wasn't my fault, why was I here?

"I know it's not you."

"What?"

"Shortly, you will be back to yourself."

I had no idea what she was talking about, but this whole Catholic thing had been a confusion since its beginning, and it was now getting to be more than I could handle. She knelt down at the opening to the pew and took both my hands in hers and demanded loudly, "Let this boy alone!" Her eyes frightened me. They were staring into my eyes as if she was trying to see my brain.

"All right," I said. "I'll leave him alone."

"Liar!" she shouted.

She pulled me to my knees at the edge of the pew.

"Now we will pray and wait for the priest." She began reciting the Our Father. I pulled my hands free and pushed between her and the edge of the wooden pew back. She grabbed for me, but I pushed her away and spun toward the back of the church. I had taken two quick running steps when I ran full force into the purple silk robes the priest had changed into. It was as if I had been a fish caught in a purple net. His hands were suddenly on my shoulders. I still couldn't understand him completely, but it sounded to me as if he was rolling off a list of saints' names. I bent his little finger with my right hand, but he was strong as a working man and held tight. My heart pumped wildly as I looked to my right to see Sister still kneeling and praying. What the hell was going on? His voice slipped in and out of English, but there was enough so I could tell he was talking to someone else other than me or Sister, and he was calling on Jesus to help him.

"Are you out of your fecking minds?" I screamed, and it echoed through the church. Off the altar, "fecking mind." Off the statues of Mary and Joseph, "fecking mind." Off the pulpit, "mind, mind, mind."

This was the same place where I sat piously on Sundays with Jake or with my sisters, in the same church where I tried to discern who was a ten-dollar giver and who was a dime giver. It was the same church where I spoke directly to Jesus and listened to his answers, the same church where the sound of the Latin Mass soothed my soul. Now this priest with the foreign accent was asking my name, and the smell of incense was making me nauseous. He sprayed holy water at me, and it ran down my face.

"Who are you?" he insisted. "What is your name?"

"My name is John Hourihan, I live at 197 Purchase Street. You know me." I turned to Sister and pleaded. "You know me, Sister."

She blessed herself in horror or guilt.

The priest had retreated entirely to his native language, leaving English totally behind. His eyes were raised to the far-off ceiling, and he continued to shout. I hauled off and kicked him in the leg with all I had, and his grip loosened for a second. As he reached for his shin, I pulled away, stepped back and stared at him. Sister continued to murmur her prayers. I made the sign of the cross. He stared at me too, for just a second, and then suddenly he looked like someone who just realized he had made a horrible mistake.

He reached out for me, but I stepped back again, "God will put you in hell for this," I shouted, refusing to let the tears escape from my eyes. I swallowed hard, blinked my eyes, turned away, and started toward the door, but since I had to walk in front of the altar, I genuflected… all the way to the floor. Then I walked out of the church, stopping only to anoint myself at the holy water receptacle. Then I walked by myself down the sidewalk past the school to Main Street. I walked alone to a place I had been before. I stepped inside the front door of the taxi stand.

"197 Purchase Street," I said. "My mother will pay you when we get there."

I went outside and climbed into the back of the taxi and waited.

## CHAPTER 28
Beginning Again

**THE NEXT DAY WAS SATURDAY.**

The June sun burned down, and the temperature had reached into the 80s, and then it edged into the 90s, and even though there were still a few days left in the school year, I would not return to school.

I was up with the sun and descended slowly, silently down the back stairs, and went out through the back door to the yard between the house and the barn. The tree branches had grown red buds and some even had the beginnings of yellowish-green leaves at their tips, and the matted grass of winter was beginning to rise again. Robins were back, and I followed one as it hopped to my rock, the big rock between the barn and the berry bushes next to the path that led to the open field. I held out my hand with Cheerios in it to the bird, and he ate some. At least he knew who I was. I laid down on the rock to feel the warmth seep into my back, and I watched a single, sad cloud crossing the blue sky. I sat up and looked around. It seemed there was no one but me awake in the world.

I cried. I didn't care if I was supposed to or not.

It appeared to me that no one, not even good people, not even the empathetic nuns and priests, not even my mother and father, not even my sainted grandmother, could keep these damn commandments. And it appeared that I was the only one trying, and the others had decided I must be possessed by a devil. I got up from my rock and walked across the driveway to the stone wall overlooking Gonhue's field, and, sitting down, I thought about Friday.

I got up and threw a rock at a bird in the tree adjacent to the raspberry bushes, the tree that marked the path into the field. No one was around, so as I often did in the woods, I thought out loud.

"They all call themselves Christians. They say they are Catholics, but they worship money and medicine more than God. They ignore us poor people, and they don't care about the hungry people except to tell them God will provide. That is just wrong."

I climbed down into the quarry hole. It wasn't that deep, and we did it all the time. I sat inside the ring of rocks we had for years called "the fort."

## Baltimore Catechism: Clean Slate (Fall and Rise of a Catholic Boy)

I started talking again. "They put people in prison and nursing homes and forget about them, and even my father and uncles take our Lord's name in vain as quickly as you can say Jackie Robinson, and they think Buster, the best guy I know, only has one name and is going to hell. People sell booze to drunks on Sunday and send them home to beat their families. They dropped an atomic bomb on Japanese kids. They collect money in the church and make money outside it on Sunday. Then they covet everything and everyone and call adultery only natural, and they don't honor their parents but do honor people who kill for us in the name of war."

I looked at a nearby tree and shouted, "My own father stole a bunch of orange juice, and my best uncle killed someone. And I bet he wasn't going to ride that horse."

The most beautiful thing I had seen in this whole year, a natural, beautiful naked body, I was supposed to be ashamed of. With all that I saw around me, that was what was deemed to be "dangerous."

I turned and ran the whole way back to the house. Inside, I retrieved *The Baltimore Catechism*, wondering just why the priest thought I was the enemy of my religion when it seemed I was the only one trying to go by its rules. I returned to the stone wall, sat on the wobbling stones, and fingered the pages of the book that I saw as the instructions for my religion and life. I decided my future while sitting on the stone wall that surrounded Gonhue's field, only one day after my attempted exorcism.

There were certain things that made sense to me. I loved this place where I lived, this 197 Purchase Street, and I loved the people who lived here with me. I loved the cedar-shingled hovel with the broken toilet and sometimes working furnace. I loved the garden with its grapes and rhubarb, asparagus, and vegetables, but not so much the dandelion leaves. I loved Butch the cat and Seabee the dog.

I loved the brook behind my house that emptied into the lily pad-covered Louisa Lake then crawled on to become the Charles River. I loved the blue summer sky, and the white winter mornings, the smell of the smoke from the chimneys, and the sound of snow shovels in the dark when the men got home from work. It had all become part of my genetics. I loved the bark of the dogs, an orange soda with Buster, and the crows answering each other across miles of woods, and I loved the friends who lived there with me. The only adventures I needed were right here in the woods, the quarry hole with the smell of birches and pine trees in the morning. I loved the taste of raw rhubarb and green grapes. It was my Garden of Eden, and I had been thrown out by life, a crazy nun, and a priest who didn't speak English.

Then there were the lies about putting me in the Britannica and sending me to China, where I would never see my mother and father and sisters and brothers again. There was the ruler to the back of my hands, and on a different day the loving empathy of the nuns and the cold discipline of the priest. There was the safety of the school and church that told me

God watched over all of us, and that He had created this world for us, and that those woods behind my house were owned by God and therefore were safe for me. My mother had told me to learn what they had to teach me, and I had stepped willingly onto the merry-go-round, but it was time to get off. They had told me that it was my call.

I decided that it didn't matter who went by the rules. I had been taught what I was supposed to do. Just like my mother and my book had told me to do, and whether I followed the rules I was taught or not was up to my free will. I learned that I was not a god but an imperfect human being and just a kid, and God didn't expect me to do it perfectly. I was just supposed to try, which I was doing.

Suddenly, my mother was sitting on the stone wall next to me. I looked at her moccasin-clad feet in the new growth of grass next to mine. I didn't look up but quickly rubbed my eyes to make sure they weren't crying.

"Are you okay?" she asked.

I nodded sadly. She waited. After a few minutes, I turned to her and said, "I know you told me to learn what they have to teach me, that it was the law, but this is all so hard."

"What's the matter?"

"I believe in God."

"Good."

"I love God, and I think God loves me."

"He does."

"I don't think I have a strong inclination to do evil."

I looked up to see her face. She chuckled. "No, I don't think so either."

"I treat everyone like I want them to treat me."

"I know. I've seen that. That's good."

"I don't have any devil in me."

"No, you don't." She put her hand on the back of my neck like my father did sometimes when we walked through certain parts of town.

She was looking straight out across Gonhue's field.

"I never did," I said.

"I know."

"Mom, no one goes by these rules." My eyes were watering, but I refused to cry.

"I know."

"But they shouldn't punish the people who try just because we mess up."

"What do you think about these rules? The ones in the book." She pointed at the blue catechism book in my lap.

I thought for a few seconds then said, "I like them. They're hard. I think you can't be a human being and go by them all the time. I'll try, but if I screw it up, it's between me and God. I'll do what God tells me." The rock was hurting my ass, so I shifted to the grass at her feet. "I'm not going to pay attention to these people any more just because I make a mistake. You'd have to be God to do all this right all the time. At least I'm trying. They aren't even trying to go by the commandments, and they aren't going to punish me anymore. I'm doing my best. Do you think that will be okay?"

"Do I think what will be okay?"

"That you, and me, and God are going to be in charge of me, not these other people, the nuns and priests and Grammy and Aunt Kathleen?"

"I think that would be preferable." She kissed me on the top of the head, stood up from the wall, and said, "Let's go have lunch."

We had a grilled cheese and a bowl of tomato soup. That was the day I became a religious person. I guess the book had worked. I guess the nuns had done their job. I believed that if God loves us, and I believe He does, then no matter what Grammy and Aunt Kathleen and all the nuns and priests say, as long as we are trying to do right, pretty much none of us is going to hell in a hand basket.

# About the Author

**John T. Hourihan Jr.,** a retired journalist, has won state, regional and national awards for his opinion column in several New England newspapers. He received the Cross of Gallantry for valor in Vietnam, where he served three tours as a Vietnamese linguist. He is disabled now from the effects of Agent Orange. He lives with his author wife Lin Hourihan (The Virtue of Virtues, The Mystery of the Sturbridge Keys) in the woods of central Massachusetts. His other works are *The Mustard Seed – 2095*, *The Mustard Seed – 2110*, *The Mustard Seed – 2130*, *Beyond the Fence: Converging Memoirs*, *Parables for a New Age I* and *II*, *Play Fair and Win*.